BUSINESS TURNAROUND BLUEPRINT

TAKE BACK CONTROL OF YOUR BUSINESS AND TURNAROUND ANY AREA OF POOR PERFORMANCE

By Fred Herbert

BUSINESS TURNAROUND BLUEPRINT

by
Fred Herbert

Business Turnaround Blueprint

Copyright © 2017 by Fred Stephen Herbert

Printed in USA

Dedication

This book would not be possible without the loving support and encouragement of my wonderful wife Tracy. She has been incredibly supportive of my mission to help business owners, through this book, and through my other initiatives.

Thank you, Sweetheart!

Foreword

When I accepted the honor to write the foreword to this amazing book, I asked Fred about what he hoped to accomplish in writing the book, and he replied, "I did feel God told me a few years ago, to help save 100,000 businesses from failure and this could help hit a large group." After having read the book, surely God will believe that Fred helped achieve HIS purpose. I sincerely think that this book has the potential of helping every leader of a small-medium sized business in the US and potentially globally.

Then I asked, "Why me?" and Fred said, "Because of your own turnaround experience." I have been a project engineer, department manager, general manager, business owner and entrepreneur. At every stop, I was either planning and executing a turnaround or closely advising others doing similar. Here is an overview of one of the more interesting turnaround challenges: I had been plucked from a large global company to come on board as the general manager to turnaround this unprofitable division. There were opportunities for improvement in each of the four separate businesses. However, we made a modest profit in year 1 and from years 2-5 we became the most profitable division in this $600 million corporation.

Each of the businesses had difficult turnaround issues, but one was exceptionally challenging. It was a $16 million manufacturing business that lost $6 million in operating profits in year 1 (although the profits in the other businesses more than offset the losses in this business). At the end of year 5 the sales were $20 million and the operating profits were $6 million (interest, corporate expenses and taxes were allocated to the overall division financial statements). That is a $12 million swing in profit in 5 years! In terms of productivity, in year 1 it took 75 employees to produce 45,000 units of production weekly. By year 5 only 45 employees could produce 75,000 units per week.

So how was this turnaround accomplished? These are some key actions:

- Laid off 100 people in entire division on one day
- Tried 3 business managers
- Reduced scrap from 40% to <5%
- Sponsored design and installation of semi-automated early stage process
- Personally, took over the leadership of the Heavy-Duty Aftermarket sales group
- Changed from individual incentive plan to group incentive plan called Improshare
- Established closer tie between manufacturing and national sales team
- Maintained minimum production with salaried personnel when union workers were on strike
- Sold surplus land and other assets

When someone asked, "How did you do this?" we replied, "We tried every idea that came into our minds." We were heroes and thought of as having accomplished the impossible. The business was saved and later combined with a similar business in Canada resulting in the biggest in this specific industry in North America.

But here is the other side of the story. This occurred before turnaround management came to be viewed as much of a skill as an art. I was effectively self-taught, and my only specific training had been the turnaround of a 700-person department in a GM assembly plant. This was indeed a major accomplishment, but it took over 4 years to accomplish the objectives. **There is no doubt that if I had had access to Fred's book and its systematic approach, the objective could have been accomplished in half the time and with greater results.** I can say with total conviction the messages and tools in the book are by far the most practical and effective that I have seen in my career.

To borrow a commonly heard phrase on TV ads – 'but there is more' – this is not just a book about the best practices in turnaround management, but rather a handbook for best management practices in general, written in an easy to understand way:

- The graphical models are great, specifically for someone like me who is more of a visual learner.
- It took me years to clearly understand the differences in the various types of plans needed by every business. Fred explains all in a succinct easy-to-read chapter.
- Depending on the severity of the turnaround situation, it may be wise for the reader to start immediately in Chapter 4 about cash flow management.
- In times of great turmoil communications become highly important, and Fred addresses the proper approaches in Chapter 5.

- Chapter 6 is on quality, and one of the great lessons I have learned is that good customers can be patient with higher prices, late deliveries or botched communications but nothing drives customers away more quickly and permanently than quality issues. Read and understand this chapter in great depth.

- Then there are clearly understandable explanations of problem-solving tools, process and system development, and financial analysis.

- Each chapter ends with tips on taking action, and a good habit would be to scan all of this material on a regular basis.

Lastly, this is a book not written by an academic but by a practical professional who has lived and experienced all that is in the writing. In whatever time that I have to devote to achieving managerial excellence in current and future entrepreneurial pursuits I will feel more confident of my success by having my personal copy of *Business Turnaround Blueprint* as a ready reference.

Mal Bass

President/Owner – SolarTex Group, LLC

Table of Contents

Introduction 1

Chapter 1 – Turnaround Mindset 5

Chapter 2 – Knowing the Truth 17

Chapter 3 – Planning 30

Chapter 4 – Cash Flow and Financial Controls 50

Chapter 5 – Communication with Stakeholders 68

Chapter 6 – Quality Products and Services 75

Chapter 7 – Customers - Getting and Keeping 86

Chapter 8 – Getting Employees Involved 106

Chapter 9 – Key Business Metrics 115

Chapter 10 – Effective Business Systems 126

Chapter 11 – Continuous Transformation 149

Chapter 12 – Funding the Turnaround 159

Conclusion 175

How I Help My Clients 176

Introduction

Before you get started in the *Business Turnaround Blueprint* chapters, I'd like to give you a little bit of introduction, give you some background, and some tips before you get started. I want you to know that this book is dedicated to helping you transform and improve your business and, in some cases, save your business. When I use the word "turnaround," I'm really talking about anything that you do to transform or improve any area of your business that's not going in a positive direction or meeting your expectations as a business owner or leader. Your business could be anywhere from on the edge of closing to just having some performance areas that are not going in the direction you'd like and wanted to improve.

The tools and principles that I teach here will help you in either situation. I have packed a lot of content into this program. Sometimes you may feel like you're drinking water out of a fire hydrant. I decided to err on the side of too much information rather than not give you enough to effectively make the changes you need in your company. You can pick and choose which chapters work best for you. I wanted to be sure you had the tools and strategies you need to turnaround your business.

A quick disclaimer; I'm not trying to make any claims or guarantees of your successful turnaround because I don't know the details of your specific situation. What I do know is these principles have been proven over time and they *will* improve any business. This is really about going back to business basics; the tools and strategies I teach here are used by all world-class organizations.

You will need to pick some focus areas because we will cover more in these chapters than you can possibly implement right away. Pick one or two items to focus on first. You may come up with 20 things that you want to do, but don't feel like you have to do it all right now. Another thing to point out is that this book is written in some cases at a very high level. Many of the concepts covered here can be very complex subjects. Each subject could have volumes of information written on them, but I have focused on giving you just a high-level overview. Every business is at a different level and a different place and will have to develop their own unique plan to implement the strategies that will work best for them.

Here is an overview of what is covered in each chapter:

- **Chapter One**, learn about the turnaround mindset that's going to help you in your journey. Also, available immediately will be **Chapter Two**, which is called Knowing the Truth. It's really about doing the business assessment of your company.

- **Chapter Three** is on turnaround strategic planning and developing your turnaround strategy.

- **Chapter Four** is about cash flow and financial controls that you can use to improve your business.

- **Chapter Five** is on how to communicate with your key stakeholders, your employees, your bankers, your creditors, and all those that you need to be in communication with about your turnaround strategy.

- **Chapter Six** is on the quality of your products and services. A lot of companies in a downturn situation let their quality and their services slip. We want to make sure that's not true for your organization.

- **Chapter Seven** we cover your customers: getting them and keeping them. Having a strong customer acquisition process and lead generation system is critical in improving the sales and revenue of your business.

- **Chapter Eight** is on getting your employees involved in your turnaround. If done properly, your employees can be the key to turning around your business and increasing performance and profitability.

- **Chapter Nine** is about your key business metrics, and making sure you're watching the numbers of your business, the numbers that can tell you exactly how you're doing and where you need to focus.

- **Chapter Ten** focuses on business systems. Making sure you have systems in place in your business that make things run smoothly and efficiently. An advantage of good business systems is that your company can run without you.

- **Chapter Eleven** is on continuous transformation. This is about creating a continuous improvement process in your organization so that you stay ahead and are always working on improving your company.

- **Chapter Twelve** is about funding your turnaround. How do we make sure you have enough cash flow for the turnaround of your company?

Need Additional Help

If after reading this book you feel you the need for additional help in developing your Business Turnaround Plan, feel free to contact me directly at:

fred@fredherbert.com

If you would like to get on my calendar to schedule a call with me to discuss your current situation and how I could help you speed up Turnaround Planning, Execution Process, or help with a Business Strategic Assessment, go to:

www.fredherbert.com/schedule

Let's dive-in and get to work!

Chapter 1
Turnaround Mindset

You might be wondering why I am starting this book by talking about your mindset. Well, you may be one of those lucky few business owners who doesn't have a problem with mindset and therefore don't need this chapter. If that's you, fantastic! Feel free to move on to the next chapter.

Most of us business owners have been affected negatively by our business struggles. The stress can be overwhelming. It saps our energy. The way we deal with our stress and our business can affect our health. It very commonly causes challenges with our relationships, and it can affect our passion for our business.

The truth is most of us need what I call our "Rocky" comeback moment. I realize that you may not be familiar with what I am talking about. In the very first *Rocky* movie, Sylvester Stallone is running up the stairs and you hear the song "Eye of the Tiger" playing. It was a very dramatic moment in the movie where Rocky turned the corner and was on the road to a comeback. A lot of us need that comeback mindset. We need that energy. We all need that comeback moment. If you haven't seen the movie or just need a little motivation then go on

YouTube and watch a clip of that movie and get your comeback energy going.

Before you embark on your turnaround journey, you need to ask yourself a few questions.

Question #1: Do you believe you can do it? - Do you have the belief system that you're going to be able to turn things around, and you're going to be able to address the struggles that you're facing in your business?

Question #2: Do you have the skills that are required? You really need to be honest with yourself.

Question #3: Do you have the help required? Whether it is from outside or internal sources, do you have the help that have the skills that are going to assist you in this journey?

Question #4: Do you have the energy required? If you're completely beat down and you have no energy, it's going to be very difficult for you to make this transition and make the turnaround steps that are required.

A major key in your turnaround effort is going to be your willingness to change and your openness to consider new strategies. Your turnaround is likely to require several paradigm shifts on how you think about things along the way. This paradigm shift may involve your employees, or even how you deal with debt and money. You may need a complete shift on how you deal with customers and your understanding of their value. It might be related to marketing and sales. You may need a shift in thinking about how you handle your processes and the systems in your business. There may be many different areas where you may need a complete shift in the way you're doing things now and the way you're thinking about things. This is why it's so important to think about your mindset.

Why is your business struggling right now?

External Factors

It could be external factors. Maybe the economy has affected your business. Maybe your industry's in a downturn. Possibly the government has impacted your industry. Whether it's from excessive regulations or taxation, the government can have an impact. It could be generational shifts. What I mean here is you could be dealing with employees of the X generation (or whatever the latest new letter is) that have different attitudes about work and you haven't been able to cope with the generational changes well. It could be available resources which could be in the area of money. For example, the banking industry has really tightened up which could affect your ability to fund accounts receivable or fund growth. Available resources could be in the way of skilled employees available in your area.

Internal Factors

Your business struggles might be related to internal factors. You could have made some management decisions that didn't pan out well, or the decisions aren't going in the right direction. You might have made some poor hiring decisions. Maybe you've taken your eye off the ball and let your quality slip in your products or services. Maybe you've been weak in your cash management and let your cash flow get out of control. It is possible you have overextended debt, made large purchases that you're having a challenge in being able to pay back. Maybe your business is simply struggling because you've had poor processes and procedures that are coming back to haunt you now.

There are many reasons why your business might be struggling, both external and internal, but the truth is, you are right now where you are. There's nothing we can do about that. The past is the past or the reasons are the reasons. For whatever the reason, you must take responsibility for engineering your own business turnaround. That's what's good about what I am covering in this book. That's why I'm so glad you're here. You've decided to take responsibility and you're ready to turnaround and improve (or even save) your business.

The Past is the Past

Let's not dwell in past mistakes. You've made some mistakes, obviously. All of us have. None of us business owners are perfect; we've all made mistakes. But don't dwell on those. Learn what you can from those mistakes so that you won't repeat them. The value you can pull out of past mistakes is what you can learn from them. Now, it's time to develop a plan. It's also important that you get whatever support you need – I will talk more about that later in this book. And of course, you've got to take action. But action is not valuable unless it's systematic. What I mean by systematic is that it's repeatable and you keep doing it. You might take an action today, but then if you let it slide, it's likely to be of no consequence. You must be systematic about taking action and we talk more about action planning and taking action later in another chapter.

Leadership

Your turnaround efforts are going to require your leadership. This book is NOT about bringing somebody in to take the bull by the horns and lead your company into a turnaround. This book IS about you, as the owner, being the leader in your own turnaround. I want you to examine right now what you can do or how you can be a better leader. You need to get input on what changes you could make that would make you a better leader. This book is all about taking action and becoming a better leader, the leader that's needed to turnaround your business.

Take Care of Yourself

Turning around a struggling business is like a marathon. That's a really good analogy for it. It takes a lot of energy and it's not an overnight thing. It's not an overnight fix. It's a marathon, so I'm suggesting you get the rest you need and take good care of your health.

When you're stressed, you're not getting the sleep you need and that's going to affect your ability to have the energy you need to turnaround your business. Work on your diet. Oftentimes when we're in a stressful situation, we're working a lot of hours; we find it difficult to eat right. And that's going to affect your ability in the long haul. Remember, we are focusing on the long stretch here. Get some exercise! Make the effort to de-stress. Figure out what strategies work best for you to de-stress your life.

Maybe you should consider getting away for a few days. I'll bet this idea hits home for you. I bet you know exactly what you need to do, whether it's eating better, exercising, or getting away. You know what you need to do. I'm encouraging you do it so that you're ready for the marathon of turning around your business.

Unpopular Decisions to Make

You will have some difficult decisions to make along the way. Be prepared to make some unpopular decisions also. You're going to have to reevaluate everything about your business. This is called zero base thinking. It means you need to forget some of the decisions you've made and why you've made them. You must make new decisions based on where you are today. Reevaluate everything. This will often require making some changes. It may be in your people or possibly in your processes. But you are going to be facing some changes and you're going to have to make those tough decisions. And you really need to ask yourself right now, are you willing to do everything necessary to improve your business? It goes back again to why mindset is so important.

Mindset Tips

- Take full responsibility. You are the business owner. You are where you are. You have to take responsibility for turning your business around. Visualize what the future is going to look like after your turnaround.
- Where do you want it to go?
- Where should it be? This goes back to planning and this is something we'll cover more later on in this book.

I'd like to recommend that you listen to audio, read books and quotes by motivational authors. Listen to Tony Robbins. Read

Napoleon Hill's *Think and Grow Rich*. Read *The Magic of Thinking Big*. There are a lot of good motivational resources that can help you. Filling your mind with that kind of information right now will help you immensely to get the motivation you need to turn around your business. I've already mentioned this before, but you must take care of your health. Use good time management strategies. Make sure you're not "majoring in the minors." Go back to the basics of time management. Make sure you're doing the things that are urgent and important, not doing things that are just urgent and unimportant. And be very results-focused. Make sure everything you're doing is moving you toward the results that you're looking for.

Make sure you're focusing on the big picture items. Are you spending your time or are you focusing your employees' energy on things that really aren't going to make a difference? You may need to change the people you're hanging around with. Make sure you're associating with motivated and encouraging people, people that build you up. Stay away from the Debbie Downers.

Reevaluate what you're personally strong in and where your weaknesses are. Focus on your strengths and consider bringing in resources that can help build you up in the areas where you're weak. Watch out for the negative self-talk. You may be beating yourself up for the situation your business is in. Stop it! Stop talking to yourself in a negative way and start being positive and moving forward in a positive direction.

It's often helpful to review your past successes. You've done a lot of things right in your business. You've done a lot of things right in many areas of your life so go back and look over the things that you've done well in the past. Write them all down.

When you get a little down about your business or where things are in your life, review this list and remember you've done a lot of things right and have had success in many areas. You can use that energy to improve your future. Take a step back by getting away for a little bit and re-evaluating where you're at: Why you started the business in the first place? What are your goals? What is your mission and vision? Take a step back and think about why you're even here.

Emotions

Keep your emotions in check. Are you prone to anger and outbursts? How are your emotions affecting your employees? How are your emotions affecting your family? Try to keep them in check. Find another venue for venting your emotions, but don't take it out on those around you, especially the employees that you're depending on to help you in your turnaround.

Be open to change and willing to develop new strategies on how you run your business. Don't let pride get in your way. The Bible says, "Pride comes before a fall." Pride can really be an issue when you're in a turnaround situation. You have to swallow your pride, face the facts, and move on with a strategy that's going to turn around your business. You're going to hear in this book a lot about getting back to business basics. You're going to read a lot of things that you already know that you have stopped doing. Go back to basics, the basics of running a successful business. You're likely going to need to work on your self-discipline. Have you been as disciplined as you need to be about how you manage your business? Have you not dealt with issues with employees as quickly as you should have?

Have you put in the hours that you know you needed to? Self-discipline is possibly an issue you need to work on.

Get Help!

Get help where needed. It goes back to knowing your strengths and weaknesses. Where do you need help in your organization? Make sure that you get help where needed. A great principle from John Maxwell, who's an expert on leadership, talks about the "Law of the lid" and that everyone needs to know where their personal lid is. Your organization is not going to rise above your level of ability. Make sure you know the areas where you're weak and get help there.

Let me reiterate a few mindset prerequisites. **Your mindset is going to be the primary determiner of your success.** I believe your mindset is going to determine how successful you are in your efforts to turn around your business. Remember, you are responsible. As a business owner, the buck stops here. You have to muster up the strength, courage and energy to turn this thing around. You've got to be open to new ideas and different business strategies, which we're going to cover in all these chapters. So try to read this book with an open mind and with the attitude that you will put away pride and seek whatever help is necessary to improve your business.

Let's face it; you've got people that are counting on you. You have your family who's counting on you to make this business turnaround work. You have employees that are counting on you for leadership. They need you to drive this bus and get this company back on track. You've got customers that rely on your products and services. You have suppliers that you're buying from that need your business. You have creditors or investors that are relying on your ability to be able to pay them back. And don't forget, you need this for yourself too.

I mentioned self-discipline earlier. Let me go into just a little bit more detail here. As I've mentioned, I think leading your turnaround is going to require a lot of self-discipline, and past habits are hard to break. The way you've been running your business and the habits you have formed in your business are often a challenge. Change is often difficult. And whether it's with yourself or your employees, new strategies will often be met with resistance. Many people are averse to change. A good little book you might get and share with your employees is called *Who Moved My Cheese*. It's a great tool in teaching change management to your employees, which I write more about in a later chapter.

It's very likely you're going to need more rigid financial disciplines as you move forward in your business. I discuss a lot about cash flow management and financial controls later in this book.

You may also need to increase employee accountability. We'll talk more about that when we get into the chapter on getting your employees involved in your turnaround process. I don't know if this is you, but a lot of business owners when their business is struggling or they're in a tough situation, are not very visible to their employees. They're down and out and they're just really not encouraging their employees enough. You need get out of the office and be more visible, you want to show commitment. You must be that consistently positive and confident leader for your business and get your employees involved.

Attitude Adjustment

The bottom line, it's very likely that you're going to need some sort of an attitude adjustment. You're going to need to display some changes in the way you look at things and the attitude you display to your employees and those around you and the people you work with and your suppliers, all your key stakeholders. You need to display and communicate hope and optimism. You must believe you're going to turn this thing around and things are going to be better. You must display that and show that you believe it. You probably need to be much more open and honest on how you communicate with others about the current state of your business. In a later chapter I cover communicating with key stakeholders. You must swallow your pride and be the person that can turn this business around. One more time, you must be willing to change.

Motivation starts with the big "W" questions, I like to call them.

- Why did you start the business in the first place?
- Why do you want to improve your business?
- What's the motivating factor? What will the desired future state look like?
- Where do you see your company going in the future (1, 5, 10 years)?
- When are you going to make the necessary changes to move your business forward?
- Who else will benefit from your successful turnaround?

As we mentioned earlier, I know your family, suppliers, employees, and your creditors are all invested in the successful improvement of your business. There are many people who will benefit from your turnaround. Keep this in mind as you work to build up the energy and the self-discipline necessary to make this turnaround happen.

Taking Action

Here are a few closing action items for you

- Be open and willing to make the paradigm shifts required to turn around your business.
- Learn what you can from what happened in the past and be ready to move on.
- Work on your leadership.
- Take care of yourself.
- Be willing to improve your self-discipline.
- Make the required attitude adjustment if you currently lack the necessary motivation.
- Know your Why's and Who's. Why are you in this business in the first place? Who is this turnaround going to impact? You have got a lot of people counting on you.

Chapter 2
Knowing the Truth

The focus of this chapter is on knowing the truth about your business. This is about doing a full business assessment, really looking at where your business is right now, and what the true current state of your business is. The truth and nothing but the truth. It can be a challenge for us as business owners to see our business as it truly is. We must be prepared to take the necessary actions to make our business better based on what we learn is "true" about our business and its current state.

What's the first step you need to take, other than what we already covered in the first chapter of having your mindset right? I believe the first step is asking a few difficult questions. We covered this a little bit in the previous chapter on mindset, but it is good to understand, how did we get to this point, and what issues are we currently facing? The real question is, what do we need to do now?

As a business owner, it's very important that you try to be objective, but that's very difficult to do. You put our own blood, sweat and tears into this business and part of your life is wrapped around the business. You probably have made all the purchasing decisions. You've hired most, if not every, employee, or you have been involved in the hiring process of every employee. You have likely been involved in the development of your products, services and processes. You're so intimately involved in your company; it's just hard to see it objectively. It's hard to really look in the mirror and see what your business really looks like.

And the fact is the truth often hurts. The first question we really need to address is, "is our current situation caused by external or internal forces (as we've talked about already)"? And another tough question that hurts is the question about you as a business owner, "has the business outgrown your ability to manage it"? I believe if a business owner is not willing to face the cold hard facts about their business situation and what it will take to save it, then there's really nothing that I can do to help them.

Knowing the truth requires an assessment tool. It really starts with what's called a gap analysis. In this gap analysis, you're going to be looking at cash flow and financials, products and services, your customers, your employees, the quality, marketing, your leadership and management system. This is just the tip of the iceberg of what you will be looking at when you do a full assessment of your business.

The Current State

Here's an example of doing an assessment on a business that has been struggling. This is what its current state looked like in graphical form. I've rated it on a scale of 1 to 10 in each of these 10 categories: financial, customer, employee, their standards, their planning process, their quality, their systems, their marketing, productivity, and their organization.

They don't plan well. They have very poor standards. They're not very organized. But they are fairly strong on their quality of products and services and also have a good strong customer base. Not too bad at marketing systems, but with some room for growth. This chart is called a spider diagram and graphed this way you can see that what could have been a nice circle is really misshaped. A company with this kind of shape is not going to run very well.

Let's go back to this company after a year or two and see how it's rated now. It's really moved up in a lot of these categories; financial is eight, customer base is eight, employees rated at a nine, and quality is a nine (it was already an 8.) Of course, they're not perfect in areas, but they have improved in many areas. And let's see how that looks in a spider diagram.

A very different picture. A company that is rated like this and has a more circular shape is more balanced. It's going to run much smoother. Now, let's compare the two together.

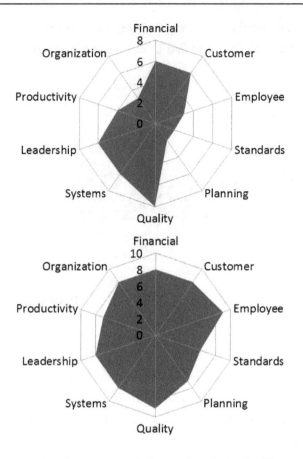

You've got the first one and then what it looks like now. A huge improvement. If you compared these to a wheel that's rolling down a street, which one of these is going to roll better? Which business would you want of these two businesses? Which one do you think is going to be more profitable? Which one is going to have better employees, stronger employees, and which one is going to give better quality service to their customers? I think you'd agree, the second one, the one on the right would be a much better company to work with, to work for, and to own.

The Turnaround Process

First, we must determine the current state of your business. In the next chapter, we will begin working on developing a plan that will include how to mitigate the gaps in your organization. These are the gaps that are discovered during this assessment process. And lastly, we take systematic actions on the plan that we've developed. All of that leads us to achieve our turnaround goals to meet the transformation and improvement goals you have for your organization. It's a simple process, but it's not easy. There's a lot of work involved in all this, but it all starts with determining your current state.

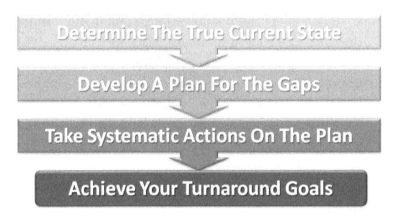

One tool that I provided in this book is a **Business Turnaround Blueprint™ Business Excellence Assessment**. You can download a copy at:

www.businessturnaroundblueprint.com/book-resources

Here's a quick shot of what it looks like.

Here's how you use the **Business Turnaround Blueprint™ Business Excellence Assessment**. Start off with giving this assessment tool to all of your key employees. You will ask them to rate your business for each question about your company on a scale of one to five. They check the box that they believe your company best fits in. You need to manage this process with anonymity. You must make sure the employees feel comfortable checking honestly and that you will not know how they personally rated the business. The next step, you need to compile the results.

When I personally take my clients through this process, I have the employees send the assessments directly to me and I pull all this altogether, and I keep all the identities confidential. What I like to do after we've compiled all the results is to bring that team together and talk about the results and say, "Why do you think so many scored us low in this area or that area?" It's a good way to get a better understanding of why people felt the way they did. Of course, when I'm working with a client, I can do this without the owner there, so I can get more honest answers about why they feel the way they do about the company. It's important to know the difference between how the average employee rates each one of these things versus how the owner scores it.

Of course, there are ways of keeping this confidential without hiring a third party. You can have one person assigned to take the printouts and then compile the information with no names attached.

Above is a sample from a company I actually worked with, compiling the scoring from the leadership team and the business owner. I use a different colored dot to show the owner's response and another color to show the overall average. In this case, you'll see the employees felt the company was better in category four than the owner did. This is a great tool that helps you see what the business owner/leader and the employees feel are weak or strong areas of the business and then it gives you a simple little gap analysis on areas to work on. After you go through this and see where you're missing the boat in some of these areas, it can help you develop some action plans with your employees on how you can improve in these areas.

Here are some sample questions from this particular assessment tool:

- Major decisions are guided by a clear vision and set of values that describes what we want our business to be and how to get there.
- Through their behavior, our senior leaders serve as role models in reinforcing the values and expectations.
- Our relationship with our customers builds trust, confidence, and loyalty.
- We have established work practices that fully utilize, empower, and satisfy our employees.
- Accomplishments are celebrated, recognized and/or rewarded.

There are many more questions in this tool, but this will give you an idea of the tone of the questions. For some of these questions, as an owner, you may not like the answers you get. You need to know how your employees feel about your organization.

The Baldrige Assessment

Another self-assessment tool I'd like for you to consider is called the Baldrige criteria. The Baldrige award is the nation's highest award for business excellence given by the President each year. You can find a lot of information about Baldrige criteria on:

www.nist.gov/baldridge/publications

I recommend that you download the most current Baldrige assessment framework and then you can use the questions and the criteria to determine some of the gaps in your organization.

Baldrige Criteria is broken up into seven different categories.

1. Leadership

2. Strategic planning

3. Customer focus

4. Measurement, analysis, and knowledge management

5. Workforce focus

6. Operations focus

7. Results

I really love this framework. This was developed over many years of studying the most successful and well-run businesses in the world and is a good model to pattern any business after. If you do the top six categories properly the results will naturally follow. Take the time to investigate the Baldrige model. It would help you improve your business.

In fact, when a company hires me to come in a do a full business assessment for them, I base a lot of it on the Baldrige Criteria and try to assess based on the seven criteria areas, along with a few supplemental ones.

Full disclosure – I may be a little biased. I have had first-hand experience with the Baldrige Program. Before I started my consulting practice I was a Quality Manager and helped the company I was working for win the Malcolm Baldrige National Quality Award. It provided me my first opportunity to travel to Washington DC and speak about my part in the Baldrige win. I was also a Malcolm Baldrige National Quality Award Examiner and twice went to Washington DC for a week of Examiner training at NIST (National Institute of Science and Technology).

Third Party Assessment

You may want to consider hiring a business consultant that can come in and evaluate all aspects of your business from a third-party point of view. One reason is they can often see things in your business that you are now blind to. I'm sure you're familiar with the old phrase, "You can't see the forest because of the trees." We get so close to our business that we're often blind to what the right next steps are and where we're weak. Sometimes we're even blind to where we're strong. It often takes someone from the outside to offer a fresh perspective.

Another value of bringing in a third party is they can often provide some expertise and experience you just don't have in your organization. If you do bring in someone from the outside to do an assessment for you, be certain they are familiar with assessing all aspects of your business.

Assessment Options

Here is a list of so of the assessment options you have available to consider:

- Self-Assessment – Using the tools described above
- Third Party Assessment – Getting that outside perspective will help get to the "Truth"
- Board of Advisors - You could have a team of business leaders that you go to that will give you that third-party view without having to hire someone, but a board of advisors is a good approach.
- Hire an Executive Coach - They may also help you see where some strengths and weaknesses are in you and your organization. Now, you might have a business consultant, not necessarily doing an assessment, but a consultant that you could talk to and that you can work with in the weak areas of your business.
- Turnaround Expert - You could bring in a turnaround expert that can both assess your current state and help you with strategies that will turn around your business.

Taking Action

This chapter requires action on your part.

- I have provided some tools and you need to determine what strategy you want to use to determine the gaps that are in your organization.
- Next, you must take action on those strategies.

- Take a look at the assessment tools I've provided and look at the Baldrige Criteria. One thing I need to mention about the Baldrige Criteria, it can be at a very, very high level and it's really designed to take organizations to the next level. Depending on where your company is at, it could be a little overkill.
- Get input from your leadership team. Get them involved in your turnaround. They often will have some of the answers that you need; make sure that you're tapping into your leadership team and your employees as resources in your whole turnaround efforts.

Even though this chapter is short, this may cause you the most work of any of the chapters because you've got to get in there and start assessing your business. Decide now. Are you going to use some of these assessment tools? Are you going to bring somebody in that can help you assess it? How are you going to go about determining where the gaps in your organization are?

Need Help?

If you find yourself struggling to find someone that can help you with an unbiased 3rd party assessment, feel free to get on my calendar to discuss your business and learn more about my **Strategic Business Assessment Services**:

www.fredherbert.com/schedule

Chapter 3
Planning

In this chapter, we cover how turnaround strategy and planning is involved in your turnaround process. There are many different types of plans a business owner needs. Of course, in this book we are focused on your need for a turnaround plan.

Other plans you need are:

- Strategic Plan – This is about setting the strategic direction for your business. The Turnaround is similar but more focused on the short term and getting your business out of its current situation. Strategic plans are more long-term focused.

- Business Plan - We all know we need that, but very few of us actually take the time to build a true business plan.

- Marketing Plan - In another chapter, I will cover developing marketing plans, something that you definitely need. Marketing can be the difference between success and failure in your whole turnaround strategy. And then you need a business continuity plan.

- Business Continuity Plan – This can include a lot of things.

  o What would happen if you died?

  o What would happen if you have a business partner, if that partner died?

  o What would happen if you lost one of your key employees?

  o What would happen if your whole IT system was shut down and you had a cyber-attack that wiped out all your computers?

  o What about a tornado or a flood, or all kinds of things that could happen in your business?

  Do you have continuity plans, plans in place that would get you back and running as quickly as possible?

Strategic Planning

Strategic planning is an organization's process of defining its strategy, its direction, and making decisions on allocating its resources to pursue this strategy, including its capital and its people.

What's different about a turnaround plan and a strategic plan? The primary difference between the two is a turnaround plan is much more short-term focused. One of the things that might be involved is what I call "cash flow triage." If you are currently in a tough cash flow position, your focus must be on bringing in cash, the lifeblood of your business. Along with that you might focus on reducing operational costs or another important focus may be on increasing revenue.

With the turnaround plan, we are focused on those things that you need to do right now to get immediate results. A strategic plan can be much more long-term focused. It could be one year, two years, three years, and beyond. Whereas, in a turnaround plan, you're focused on today, this week, this month, this quarter, and this year.

I will cover the strategic planning process in this book at a very high level. To give credit where it is due, this is the strategic planning process that was used by the company I worked with when we won the Malcolm Baldrige National Quality Award. It is a fantastic model and I have used it with my consulting clients to take them through the Strategic Planning Process.

The Ten Step Strategic Planning Process
- Step 1 – Planning
- Step 2 – Evaluate, Review & Assign
- Step 3 – Vision, Mission, & Values
- Step 4 – Environmental Scan
- Step 5 – SWOT Analysis
- Step 6 – Organizational Strategies (Goals)
- Step 7 – Develop Short and Long-Term plans
- Step 8 – Create Balanced Scorecard
- Step 9 – Communicate Strategic Plan to all Employees
- Step 10 – Review

The first step is planning. You actually have to develop a plan for your whole strategic planning process.

Step two is to evaluate, review, and assign. Many times, you'll be evaluating your previous strategic planning process. What do you need to do? Who's responsible? And you make those assignments.

Step three is to revisit your vision, mission, and values. You don't really have to change that every year, but you do have to look at it and decide whether any changes need to be made in this category.

Step four is environmental scan. We'll talk more about that.

Step five is doing a SWOT analysis.

Step six is developing organizational strategies and goals.

Step seven is to develop short- and long-term plans. Again, with the turnaround plan, you will be focused more on the short term.

Step eight is to create a balanced scorecard.

Step nine is to communicate a strategic plan to all of your employees.

Step ten is to review. That means we will establish a systematic review process to look monthly or quarterly at how we're doing on the action plans we created. We must not waste the effort of creating a strategic plan, put it on a shelf, and never look at it again.

Here's a high-level view of the strategic planning process.

Environmental Scan	SWOT Analysis

Mission – Vision – Values

Strategic Objectives	Strategies

Action Plans

Systematic Review

We have environmental scans and a SWOT analysis that feed into our vision, mission, and values. These feed into developing our strategic objectives and our strategies, which then flows into developing action plans, and at the end we develop a systematic review process. This is what the whole strategic planning process looks like.

Vision, Mission, and Values.

Here is an academic description of what these mean.

- Vision defines the desired or intended future state of a

specific organization or enterprise in terms of its fundamental objective and/or strategic direction. Bottom line, what do you want your company to look like in the future?

- Mission, this defines the fundamental purpose of an organization or an enterprise, basically describing why it exists. So really, what is your company all about? Why are you in business? What are you trying to accomplish?

- Values are the beliefs that are shared among the stakeholders of your organization and these values drive your culture and your priorities. So really, what are the core values of your organization?

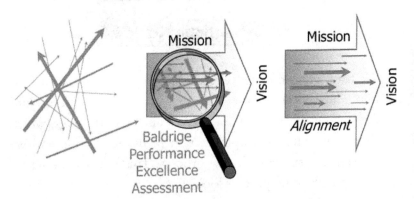

Above is an image that comes from the Baldrige Criteria that gives a good graphic example of how disjointed our plans often are. And we're not going in the right direction, some are going in the opposite directions and they're not aligned. Our desire is to get our mission, our vision, and our values aligned and going the same direction, heading for the same purpose.

Environmental Scan

An environmental scan is a great tool to take into your Strategic Planning Process. Here you begin to gather information about events, trends, and relationships in an organization's external environment. The knowledge you gain here will assist you and your management team in planning the organization's future course of action.

The environmental scanning involves the following analysis:

- Government
- Legal
- Technology
- Ecology
- Socio-cultural
- Suppliers
- Labor supply
- Service providers
- Stakeholders

During the environmental scanning process, you will obtain both factual and subjective information on the business environment in which a company is operating or considering entering.

When I work with companies to assist their Strategic Planning Process, I will normally assign members of the leadership team different areas or the Environmental Scan to research and report on during the off-site Strategic Planning Meetings.

SWOT Analysis

This stands for strengths, weaknesses, opportunities, and threats. Let's look at each of these.

- Strengths are those attributes of your organization that are helpful in achieving your objectives.
- Weaknesses are those attributes that are harmful in your ability to achieve your objectives.
- Opportunities are some external conditions that can be helpful for you to achieve your business objectives.
- Threats are some external conditions, a lot of those things that we talked about possibly in an Environmental Scan that can really damage your business performance in the future.

The SWOT analysis is a very important tool in your organization. It's very important that you and your employees work together on a SWOT analysis. When I lead a company through strategic planning, this is almost always one of the hubs of the whole plan in determining strengths, weaknesses, opportunities, and threats, and looking at how we can develop strategies around those. We want to work on our strengths, mitigate our weaknesses, look for opportunities, and be prepared for threats.

Balanced Scorecard

A tool that I believe every business needs to understand and create is a Balanced Scorecard. Here's the academic definition:

"The balanced scorecard is the performance management approach that focuses on various overall performance indicators, often including customer perspective, internal business processes, learning, and growth, and financials, to monitor progress toward organization's strategic goals. Each major unit throughout the organization often establishes its own scorecard, which in turn is integrated with the scorecards of other units to achieve the scorecard for the overall organization."

That is a mouthful. But to sum it up, we're talking about making sure that we create a scoring system that looks at the whole organization. We must not focus on one performance indicator, from one department, or from one area of the business. We want a balanced approach. We must be careful not to overlook any metric that's important to the overall business.

A balanced scorecard approach usually has four primary perspectives:

- The first perspective is financial. What are the key metrics in the financial arena?
- Another set of metrics will be on the internal business processes.
- A third is learning and growth. What is the human focus or learning the developmental areas of your business?
- And the fourth area, metrics around the customer. Things like customer satisfaction, customer acquisition, reduced customer complaints, etc.

Do a search on Google and you'll see many different examples of balanced scorecards that you can pattern yours after. The idea is that you take some objectives, measures, targets, and initiatives around the customer, around internal, around education, around finance. These are all at a very high level.

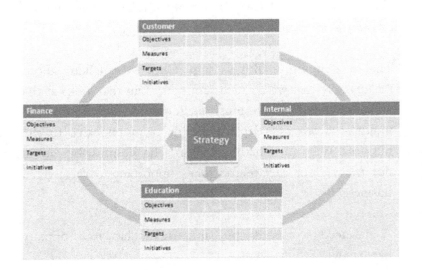

The idea of a balanced scorecard is like the dashboard of your car that clearly shows you the main things you need to be aware of as you drive. You don't need to see every light or every indicator, but you need to know the speed, you need to have an oil light, maybe your RPMs, and you need to know where your gas gauge stands. What are the key indicators that your business is running well? That's what you put on a balanced scorecard.

Action Planning

A key part of the Business Turnaround Blueprint™ Program that I'm taking you through here is the importance of a good action planning process. Without a good action planning process, your improvements will not be sustainable.

So here are a few basics of an action planning process. First, you must establish measurable milestones. It can't be a vague goal. It has to be something that you can put your arms around. You must break down the actions required to reach each goal. Then you must assign the task to someone that will be responsible to make sure the goal is accomplished. You must establish due dates and hold them accountable to meet them.

Next, you need to create a systematic review process so that you're looking at those action items and make sure you're accomplishing things on the dates they are due. If for some reason you and your team are not meeting deadlines, you may need to reestablish realistic deadlines with those resources or maybe even get additional resources, or find a new person to be responsible for a task. I'm sure you've heard all this before, but are you doing it? Objectives need to be specific, that you can see measurable results that are produced while implementing that strategy. In the process of identifying the objectives, keep asking, "As an organization are we sure we can do this?"

The third item is to integrate the current year's objectives as performance criteria in each implementers job description and performance review. I'm sure you've heard the saying, "What gets measured gets done." What I'm trying to say here is make sure employees know that achieving goals, achieving their action items is part of their job and make it a part of their review process. This helps the employees' motivation on achieving the goals that you agree on. Please remember that objectives and timelines are sometimes arbitrary and they're not really rules set in stone. You can deviate from them, but if you do need to deviate, make sure it's understood why. We're not trying to use these goals and objectives as whips. This is just a tool to make sure that we have the appropriate amount of flexibility, but don't be so flexible that nothing ever gets done.

Provided with the purchase of this book is the **10-Step Strategic Planning Process Report** which goes into a lot more detail in each of these areas. You will find charts to fill out for the Environmental Scan and more detail on how to establish Vision, Mission, and Values. There's also more detail about creating a SWOT analysis, developing strategies, short- and long-term plans, the balanced scorecard, and much, much more.

Download the **10-Step Strategic Planning Process** document at:
www.businessturnaroundblueprint.com/book-resources

Business Planning

I mentioned earlier that you need a business plan but very few businesses have one. If you are going to write a business plan, I recommend that you go to the SBA website and look at their plan outline. It gives you some really good guidelines on what needs to be covered.

Since the SBA and other resources do such a good job of helping you build a good working business plan, I will leave that to them and suggest you look into those resources.

Many people have said, "Why plan, it's all going to change anyway." It is true that plans are never perfect and will have to evolve along the way, but the mere act of planning helps you prepare for the unexpected and move your business in the direction of your choosing.

Marketing Plan

I also mentioned earlier the need for marketing plans. You might be thinking, "Why do I need a marketing plan for the turnaround of my business?" The primary reason is that sales can help you recover from many business mistakes. You can do a lot of things wrong in your business but if you know how to sell, you can almost always recover.

I believe that a consistent marketing plan can fill in those gaps when sales might normally slip. This is something I learned the hard way many years ago. My business would have months after months of really good profit, but it would only take a couple of poor months to wipe out a whole year's worth of profitability. I learned then how important it was to have a consistent marketing process. The truth be told, it may be because of the lack of marketing that your business is currently struggling. Be aware that a good strong marketing focus can make the difference and how quickly you turn around your business.

Let me give you one caution though about increasing revenue. You're probably wondering "How can increasing your sales hurt your turnaround?" Well, the simple answer is (I've seen this over and over again) increased sales can hurt you in two categories. If those sales are at a very low profit margin and if you have to carry those sales in accounts receivable. In a turnaround situation, you don't want sales for sales' sake. It needs to be profitable and give you very good cash flow.

Marketing will be covered in greater detail when we get into that chapter. But I will mention here that you do need to understand and be able to articulate your unique selling proposition. You must understand your target market. Exactly, who is the customer that you're after? Be sure that you can articulate all the benefits of your products and services. A very important part of your plan is to have defined how you're going to position your products and services against the competition.

With marketing plans you will determine the key marketing methods you're going to use in your business. Another part of your plan is to determine how you're going to market your business, and methods and processes you will use in your marketing. You need to set aside someone in your organization (maybe you) to be accountable for making sure the marketing strategies and plans that are developed are carried out. You need to develop key metrics that you're monitoring. Examples might be how many sales calls a day are being made, how many phone calls a day are being made, and so on. There are a lot of metrics related to sales. You need to determine which metrics will help you know that you're meeting your goals and that your marketing strategies are being implemented.

I have thrown out the word "systematic" several times and will again I'm sure. Being systematic is a key to your success. You can't just have a marketing strategy for a month or a quarter. You have to be systematic about it. Make sure that your review process is systematic. That it's not just a one-hit wonder and then you let it die. Part of being systematic is a regular review process. Hold people accountable and review it regularly.

Business Continuity Plans

I will touch briefly on Business Continuity Planning. What you need to do is determine all the potential business risks that you have and you want to plan for all possible disasters. You can work with your employees to help develop these plans. I like to recommend that you actually have a written continuity plan so if something does happen, a disaster falls, you've got something to look at. There are people that are experts in continuity planning who can also help you. You should consider bringing in an expert if the size and complexity of your business warrants it. A plan is no good if you don't keep it current. Be sure you're covering all the possible natural disasters: Flood, cyber-attack, fire, earthquake, tornadoes, etc.

Let me cover just a few of the common business risks:

- Death and disability of key personnel, including the owner
- Divorce of the owner
- Lawsuits
- Mechanical failure, things like the elevator not working, the heater, the air out, water line breaks, etc.
- Short-term power loss. We are now so dependent on technology that a short-term power loss can really devastate our business.
- IT system failure. How robust is your IT system?
- Have you got plans in place where you try to mitigate the risk of key personnel leaving and taking your key customers with them?
- What about the loss of a key customer? Have you planned for that?
- What about a forced location change or loss of records?
- What if you had a fire and you lost all your records? Do you have a backup system?
- You may not have thought of this, but what about the loss of a key supplier? Do you have a supplier that, if they went out of business, it would really affect your business?

These are all things to keep in mind when you're looking at business continuity plans. I don't want to depress you, but I do want you to be thinking ahead. Think about these things in your planning process.

Action Planning System

No amount of planning will be of value to a business owner if it's not deployed with an effective action plan process. Surely by now you get the point that I am a big believer in action plans. Action planning typically includes deciding who is going to do what, by when, and then what order for the organization to reach its strategic goals. It's as simple as that. As discussed on strategic planning, it is important to develop action plans around every major function of the organization: Marketing, Operations/Manufacturing, Development, Finance, Personnel, etc. Every key area of your organization will need action plans. I believe that you should ensure that each manager and also each employee are assigned (or goals linked to) action plans that contributes to the overall organization.

Consider this following example of format that you can use with an action plan:

Strategic Goal	Strategy	Objective	Responsibility	Timeline
1. (Goal #1)	1.1 (first strategy to reach Goal #1)	1.1.1 (first objective to reach while implementing Strategy #1.1)	(who's going to accomplish that objective)	(when the implementer is going to be accomplish that objective)

On the left, you have your overall strategic goal. The second box is the strategy that's associated with that goal. The next one is the objective that you need to reach while implementing the strategy. The fourth box is for who is responsible for accomplishing the goal or objective. The last box is the timeline. When is the implementer going to accomplish this objective?

46

If you would like a template that I use for Action Planning go to: www.businessturnaroundblueprint.com/book-resources

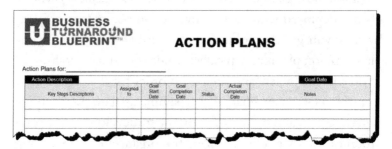

Let me go over this tool in more detail. At the very top, you say, "This is an action plan for John Doe." What is the action description and what's the goal date? And then you get John to look at what the key steps are. Some of these steps may be assigned to other people, who get assigned a goal date, goal completion date status, actual completion date, and any notes. This is a good framework for you to start with and then evolve it from here. I hope this helps.

A very important key is to have regularly scheduled action planning meetings. Here are some recommendations. Managers and supervisors should meet weekly with employees, especially the employees that have action plans associated with them and that they review the progress on those action plans. The role of managers and supervisors is to remove any obstacles (if possible) that are causing that employee to struggle in accomplishing that action item. During those meetings, you reinforce the importance of accomplishing those goals and how they affect the overall strategy of the organization. In addition, you should make sure the employee has the skills required to meet and accomplish that goal. Sometimes you will find that that action item may have been assigned to the wrong person. It's also possible you need to assign additional resources to help when an action item turns out to be much more difficult or time consuming than first thought.

I recommend that you hold monthly Action Plan Review meetings, especially with your managers, and you look back at how those actions plans are being accomplished and if they are meeting the goals of the organization. Tie this process back in with your whole strategic planning process and then your turnaround planning process.

Taking Action

Here are some action items to take away from this chapter:

- Begin right now on your turnaround strategy process. You may need to focus right now on triage, those things that will stop the bleeding, especially cash flow. Maybe there are other areas of your organization that you've got to focus on now. Go ahead and do that, but don't forget that after you get through the triage, you want to then work on the other areas of growing and improving your business.

- Go ahead and do a SWOT analysis. Get your employees involved. I like to hand every key employee a SWOT analysis worksheet and say, "Work through this." Give them a little training about SWOT analysis and then ask them, "Tell me, what you think are the strengths and weaknesses of our company? What do you think are some threats? What are some opportunities?" Get your employees involved. And then set those goals.

- Start working on developing your Balanced Scorecard. Whether you use the tool I provided or you develop your own, create an action planning tool and a review process.

Be consistent. It's very possible that you've had these kinds of processes in place in the past and you just didn't consistently keep it up. I'm encouraging you to get back at it, make this a regular part of how your business operates.

Chapter 4
Cash Flow and Financial Controls

In this chapter, we're going to be talking about cash flow and financial controls. This may be one of the most important chapters in the entire book. I am sure as a business owner you realize by now how important cash flow is. When we're talking about cash flow management, it's very important that we really understand the true value of cash, which is the lifeblood of your business.

I once heard someone give it a good analogy that a business without cash is like a car without gas. It may look pretty but it is not going anywhere. Negative cash flow issues have caused the failure of many companies. A high percentage of companies that fail are because of cash flow. Negative cash flow issues create a great deal of stress for the business owner, employees, suppliers, and all the key stakeholders.

Cash Flow Assessment

If your business is struggling at all with cash, the first place to start is with a Cash Flow Assessment. To do a Cash Flow Assessment of your business, you first have to evaluate what your current situation is. For this you may need some outside help unless you have the skills within your organization. It's often good to bring in a third party to help you do a Cash Flow Assessment. That may be your CPA, you might bring in a business consultant that could help, or even a very experienced bookkeeper.

You first have to evaluate where your money is going. Look back at least for the last 12 months and for each of your expenses (make sure that you categorize them). Then look for areas of your business that are much higher than expected. For example, you might be surprised that employee expenses are 30% of sales or that employee benefits are 12% of sales. There might be some surprises there and it's always good to categorize and look for areas that are higher than you anticipated.

Industry Standards

There are many industries that have standards that you can compare you company with to get a feel for where the top performers are in terms of financial metrics. If you belong to any industry associations they will often take member surveys that you can access and compare your company against. Another option is to ask your banker to look your industry up in some of their resources and take a look at how your business stacks up against the industry. If available, I recommend you compare your financial metrics with the top 10% to 25% in your industry. Next, look for areas that you really need to dig in deeper and may require some more evaluation. This may mean you need to drill deep into a particular category (look through all the expenses) and try to figure out where the money is going and what you can do to reduce some of those areas.

Cash Flow Triage

When your cash flow in in real trouble I like to dig in immediately and do what I call "Cash Flow Triage." By the word "triage" I mean the medical analogy of how you stop bleeding, or how you take immediate action to keep things from getting worse than they already are. The first place I like to start is to try to encourage you to do some zero-based thinking. I want you to ask yourself this question, "Knowing what I know now, would I still make the same decisions?" Especially with all purchases. You may not be able to go back and change things but at least learn from the analysis of your cash flow and where the money is going.

Here are some examples of questions you might ask yourself that could help you reduce cash:

- Would I hire this person again?
- Are they really adding value to the organization?
- Would I make the same purchases?
- Do I really have to have this item?

Take a look at your inventory. I'll talk more about inventory later but are there some assets you could sell that are taking up warehouse space? How about leases? Are you leasing anything like cars, copiers, etcetera that you could do without, especially in a time where cash is so tight? Are you members of any clubs or organization that really don't increase revenue? They're nice to be a part of, but really scrutinize, is it needed now?

Do you have some clients that are really draining your cash flow? Maybe they are not paying well, or possibly you are pricing them in a way that they are no longer profitable.

Scrutinize your clients closely and make the tough decisions needed to be made there. I have worked with many companies that failed to raise prices on the clients for years for fear they would lose them and got to the point that they would no longer be profitable.

What about the marketing strategy? Are you doing some things in marketing that may not be giving you return on your investment or you can't prove that they are? Here too I have seen many companies throwing good money after bad on marketing efforts that were not effective and costing the company money. Cut out any marketing and advertising cost that is not actually helping you acquire new clients in a cost-effective manner.

How about taking a look at your vendor relationships? Do you have some vendors that you've been working with for many, many years but they are not really giving you the best price? Evaluate your vendors at this time and make sure you are getting the best possible pricing and terms. Here is another place I have seen some big mistakes. If you are not keeping vendors honest and price shopping you are likely not getting the best possible deal. There are also times that purchases go to vendors that are liked personally and price is not looked at. Now is the time to look.

Look at any current projects you are involved in. Do you have any projects in your organization that should (or could) be either eliminated or put on hold? When cash is poor you need to reevaluate all the projects that going on right now. An example I have seen is a company in the middle of spending $6 million on new equipment and expansion when the downturn struck and they lost some big contracts they were counting on. They proceeded anyway and ended up bankrupting the company. That expansion project cost them the company, a family fortune, and hundreds of lost jobs.

This is an incomplete list but it gives you some idea of the things that you're going to scrutinize in a very tight cash situation. Another suggestion that I have found that works for many organizations is for the owner to personally sign every check that goes out the door. You may have delegated a lot of things, but if right now you are in a tight cash situation, make sure that you personally know every penny that's being spent in your organization.

I would also recommend that you review every credit card statement, bank statement, and petty cash. Look them over closely and make sure there's nothing going out of the organization that you don't personally know about and that you feel is necessary. Consider enacting a policy to personally approve every expense, say over $100, over $500, or whatever you feel comfortable with, but pick a limit that makes sense for your situation. We're going to talk about this more in a minute, but be sure that you're looking out for employee theft.

Cash Flow Projections

Now we're going to cover the value of doing regular cash flow projections. I believe, especially at a time in your organization when cash is tight, you need to be doing cash flow projections. It can be done with a simple Excel spreadsheet or even by hand for that matter. You fill out where your beginning cash is, what expected sales will be, what receivables you expect to come in, and look at your expenses that you expect in the near future. It helps you predict what your cash flow is going to look like in the next few weeks.

When it comes to creating cash flow projections, establish a time period that works best for your company. I like weekly or biweekly. If you got out as far as monthly it gets much harder to predict and is a less valuable tool. Start by estimating your incoming cash by looking at your accounts receivable report and also base your predictions on real customer payment history. Don't just put in the number that your accounts receivable report shows what is due by a certain date, but look at your customers and see how they typically pay. If it's due on the 10th but they don't usually pay 'til the 20th, don't put it down by due date, put it down by the realistic expected date. Then look at what kind of cash sales you expect, based on history or based on known orders in process. Now estimate your outgoing cash. Look at your accounts payable report and what you have to pay in the time period you're looking at. Next look at what payroll expenses are going to be over that same time period. Also take into consideration business taxes such as estimated taxes, payroll, sales, and state taxes.

Weekly Cash Flow Projection
Your Company, Inc.

CASH RECEIVED	6/26	7/3	7/10	7/17	7/24	7/31
Beginning Cash Balance	$24,250	$54,500	$60,666	$57,394	$51,943	$64,464
Cash Sales	$33,500	$37,500	$32,000	$27,500	$36,000	$42,200
Receivables Collected	$49,000	$61,540	$61,095	$52,502	$63,231	$54,285
Other Cash Received					$10,000	$18,908
Total Cash Available	**$106,750**	**$153,540**	**$153,761**	**$137,396**	**$161,174**	**$179,857**
CASH DISBURSED						
Salaries and Wages	$14,750	$14,750	$14,750	$15,855	$15,855	$15,855
Lease/Mortgage	$11,750					
Insurance		$11,085				
Office Supplies	$5,500	$3,505	$3,505	$4,088	$2,970	$4,088
Utilities				$6,693		
Repairs and Maintenance	$4,500	$4,155	$4,155	$5,117	$4,546	$5,117
Operating Supplies	$3,000	$3,950	$3,950	$2,862	$3,765	$2,862
Professional Fees			$1,575			
Commissions	$13,500	$12,850	$12,850	$12,543	$15,043	$12,543

If you would like a sample template of a Weekly Cash Flow Projection spreadsheet that I use you can find it at:

www.businessturnaroundblueprint.com/book-resources

Accounts Receivable Controls

If in your business, you give your customers credit and give them time to pay you back, the Accounts Receivable is likely an issue for you (at least from time to time). I have worked with many businesses and I have yet to find one that has managed Accounts Receivable effectively and not let it become an issue to challenge their cash flow.

This is the first thing that really hurt me when I first got into business and realized how important controls on Accounts Receivable were. I will never forget the meeting with my CPA. I went in with the question of "Why do I show a good profit but can't seem to scrape up enough cash to pay my bills?" This is when he explained that all my cash was loaned out to customers and that I was paying my payroll and material cost long before I received payment from my customer.

If your Accounts Receivable is out of control, here are some recommendations for you to consider:

- Require credit approval before shipment. Don't just give credit to someone just because they placed an order. Make sure they're credit-worthy before you give them your product or service. If they're not paying on time or they have a poor credit rating, keep them on a cash-only basis and make no exceptions for that.

- It's very important that you make sure your invoices are accurate. When people want an excuse to slow pay, they often will use invoice errors as the reason not to pay, and so you'll go back and forth for weeks trying to get invoices accurate and this really delays them paying. Make certain you have a timely and accurate billing system.

- If you're the type of business that bids on contracts, make sure you really closely review all the contract terms before you accept any bid projects. Sometimes they'll have small clauses in the bid documents where they'll hold back a lot of cash until the end of a project, and this could hurt your cash flow for months.

- As an owner, make sure you authorize all credit memos. Make sure employees are not giving credit memos out that are not approved by you and that are really justified.

- In conjunction with Accounts Receivable controls, I'd recommend that you audit invoices on a regular basis. Make sure invoices are going out promptly. I have worked with companies that were very lackadaisical about getting invoices out which caused severe cash flow issues. Make it a practice and a goal for same day invoicing. Try to bill the minute a product is shipped or project completed.

- Send out statements every month, timely and consistently. Show your customers what they owe and remind them when it's due. If an invoice is due on the 10th and it hasn't come in by the 15th, send out a past due statement. Keep a tight control of your accounts receivable.

- I highly recommend that you call past due customers weekly. You've heard the term squeaky wheel, when it comes to collection, it works. I also recommend that you turn over collections after 90 days. If they haven't paid you in 90 days your odds of collecting are greatly reduced. I've mentioned this already but I believe you should only give credit to very financially strong companies and be very quick to cut off slow-paying clients. Put them on COD very quickly. Make sure you initiate a very good credit collection system, frequent mail reminders with late charges and frequent follow-up phone calls as already mentioned.

- Another thing that could help your cash flow is to offer discounts for early payments. I have often used this strategy that really helps cash flow when implemented properly. What I do is raise my prices a little bit and then I offer a discount back for paying cash up front. Many customers that had good cash flow would take advantage of this, our cash flow was dramatically improved and I still made the same amount of money.

Put these consistent policies in place and keep them up in both good and bad times.

Employees and Cash Flow

My big concern here is in preventing employee theft. It's very important that you follow generally accepted accounting practices and limit the number of employees that have control over anything related to cash. Be sure that you segregate duties well and limit signers on your checking account. I highly recommend that only you, as an owner, can sign checks. If that's not practical, you're going to have to scrutinize the signers very closely. As the owner, you need to review monthly processed checks closely. Have your bank send your bank statements to your home and look 'em over closely.

The same with credit card statements, look them over very closely every month to make sure there are no unexpected charges on there. If anything raises a flag, talk to your employees about it and find out what's going on. I have done this on even very small items. They may turn out legitimate but the very act of looking and asking sends a signal to the employees that you are on top of expenses and will not let anything slide. Make sure that any employee who has access to credit cards is using it properly.

Consider having your CPA or some other third party do periodic audits of your accounting practices. I recommend that you do background checks on all your employees. This would include credit checks. Employees that are in deep debt and in financial trouble are much more likely to have a theft issue. One thing I've seen in many businesses I have consulted with is to have employees that over time develop an entitlement mentality. This allows them to rationalize almost anything. When they feel entitled, they don't think you're paying them enough or they can come up with all kinds of reasons why theft is logical and reasonable in their own mind.

If you have inventory, make sure you're closely monitoring inventory shrinkage. A good financial metric to watch is your material ratios. Make sure material and inventory expenses are staying consistent. Watch for spikes and if you have a spike, figure out why by digging in further and understanding what went on differently that month.

You might find a purchase order system is beneficial if you don't already have one. Make sure all your vendors know that you don't pay any invoices without a signed PO and they'll get in the habit of only sending product that has a purchase order number. Another very effective control is to reconcile all your packing slips, your purchase orders, and invoices promptly. Make sure that your invoices match the PO and the delivery receipt exactly. Sometimes you will find huge errors with them not shipping exactly what they invoice for.

If you can eliminate it, get rid of petty cash. If not, track it very closely. If possible, reduce the use of manual checks and watch for missing and voided checks.

Employee Theft

When it comes to employee fraud, or employee theft, you have a three-legged stool of:

- Rationalization
- Opportunity
- Pressure

If they have personal pressures, they can rationalize their need for stealing company assets. Add to that opportunity and you've left that door wide open. At this point they're much more likely to steal from your organization. The truth is, a disgruntled employee is much more likely to steal. You've heard the saying trust but verify? Make sure you have a verification process in place to make sure all your employees are worthy of the trust you've given them.

Pricing Products and Services

Is this you?

- Have you not raised your prices in years because you're afraid your customers just might leave and go somewhere else?
- Are you not articulating your value proposition to your customers and they are not aware of why you're worth maybe more than a competitor?
- Is your pricing dictated by your competition?
- Do you just follow the leader?

These are all questions you might ask yourself when it comes to pricing your products and services.

So here are a couple of calls to action related to pricing. This goes in the area of sales and marketing, but it also fits well in pricing. You must understand your USP, your Unique Selling Proposition. I recommend that you review all your pricing and raise prices wherever possible. I remember the first time I raised my prices. I was afraid if I raised my prices 10% I would lose a large chunk of my customers. In this particular case, I raised my prices and I lost no customers. So, that 10% just increased my profit margin dramatically.

Look over your products and services and remove anything that's unprofitable. Try to get rid of things that are not giving you a return. I will never forget when I first used a computer spreadsheet in the early 1980s to create an estimating tool. I used a time and materials formula and found there were many services I was losing money on. I quickly either raised the prices or eliminated it altogether. At the time I simply based all my prices on either industry standards or my competitors' prices. This is not an effective pricing strategy. Dig deep and know all your fixed and variable costs to determine if your product and service is profitable.

Inventory Management

Many service organizations do not have an issue with inventory, but this section is for those of you who have inventories and where storing parts and/or products is a part of your business model. Here are a few common issues that come along with inventory management.

One issue that is very common is just-in-case purchases. This is buying 10% or 20% more of a product to store it in the office or warehouse, just in case you might need it someday.

Another issue I see is purchasing extra just to get special discounts. Logic is like "Oh I only need 50, but if I buy 500, I get it 10% off." Buy just the 50. Those special discounts can cost you in the end.

I have also worked with clients that have a habit of not returning unneeded or damaged items during a restocking period. You order something, it comes in, it's got a nick, or whatever, and you take too long to go about sending it back. Or maybe you're worried about paying a 10% restocking fee for something you bought that was not needed after all. Pay the restocking fee; in a lot of cases it's better than keeping it in your warehouse for months and months.

Inventory creep is another issue I have had clients struggle with. Here's a client that I worked with that is a perfect example of this issue. Over a 10-year period, they let their inventory raise every year until they had a huge inventory. The problem was, even though the books showed an inventory value of about $120,000, it was probably only worth about $30,000 because it was all old and obsolete or damaged.

Be careful with year over year inventory creep. Here are just a few recommendations that I put in place with this client and others that have really helped. You might create a bonus program for employees to incentivize them to utilize some of the old inventory. You might find a wholesaler that will come in and buy up older obsolete inventory. Even if it's 10 or 20 cents on the dollar, it might be better to get that cash now and get it out of the warehouse.

Be sure you revisit all your purchasing strategies, and do this often. Make sure you get completely away from the old cycle of letting inventory continue to creep. And be sure to train your employees on the value of inventory, and help them to understand that inventory is cash sitting in the office or warehouse that could pay their checks or even pay bonuses (make it about something that they can benefit from). Develop a process to review inventory before purchasing anything new.

I've seen this over and over again, where employees continue to buy new inventory items when the warehouse had adequate supply. Because of a poor inventory system though, they had no idea.

GAAP (Generally Accepted Accounting Principles)

The definition of GAAP: *"The common set of accounting principles, standards, and procedures that companies use to compile their financial statements. GAAP is a combination of authoritative standards set by policy boards, and simply the commonly accepted ways of recording and reporting accounting information."*

Here are some advantages of following GAAP:

- First, you're going to be speaking the same language that bankers and CPAs speak.
- By following these practices, you create financial reports that help you understand your current business condition.
- You can use your balance sheets and income statements to monitor metrics and ratios and compare them against industry standards.
- It simplifies tax preparation for your CPA.
- If you're audited, it will smooth things out with the IRS.
- You can bring in any experienced bookkeeper and they can follow your system.

Financial Ratios

You need a very good bookkeeping system to even have financial ratios that you can monitor. Here are four categories of financial ratios:

- Liquidity Ratios
- Safety Ratios
- Profitability Ratios
- Efficiency Ratios

Your liquidity ratios are those ratios that show you your capacity to pay debts. Two common ones are your current ratio and your quick ratio. These are really cash flow ratios. Your banker and your investors will look very closely at these two ratios.

The next ratio we'll look at is safety. This is your company's vulnerability to risk. You would look here at your debt-to-equity ratio, or your debt-to-coverage ratio. This will give your banker and investors an idea of how overextended you might be.

Another type of ratio is your profitability ratio. These would be looking at things like sales growth, the cost of goods sold against sales, your gross profit margins, your SG&A (selling, general and administrative to sales ratios), net profit margin, a return on equity ratio, and return on assets.

As a business owner, you need to understand your ratios, and your metrics, and make sure that you're watching them closely. I guarantee you, your bankers and your investors will.

Some of the key ratios I like to look at in the Profitability and Efficiency categories are:

Profitability

- Sales Growth
- COGS (Cost of Goods Sold) to Sales
- Gross Profit Margin
- SG&A (Selling, General, and Administrative) to Sales
- Net Profit Margin
- Return on Equity
- Return on Assets

Efficiency

- Days in Receivables
- Accounts Receivable Turnover
- Days in Inventory
- Inventory Turnover
- Sales to Total Assets
- Accounts Payable Turnover

Taking Action

Here are some action items to take away from this chapter:

After reviewing the recommendations that we just covered, I recommend that you pick three things that will have the quickest impact on your cash flow and take immediate action on those items. As an owner, you've got to take control of your situation.

Remember my triage analogy. You've got to stop the bleeding. You've got to get in there and change things. I recommend that you make an effort to understand your limitations and get help in the areas where you are weak.

You may have more of a sales personality and don't understand the financials or the operations. If so, bring in someone that's more skilled in those areas. Or the opposite may be true. You may be like me. I am much stronger operationally and always struggled with marketing. I have hired others to help me in marketing. Bring in others that can help you in the areas that you're weak. We can't be specialists in everything.

Chapter 5
Communication with
Stakeholders

This chapter is about communication with your very important key stakeholders. It's very common that when times get tough, as business owners, we begin to clam up and not really share much with our stakeholders. When you stop communicating with your stakeholders, it causes a lot of issues. I'll share with you some ideas about communication that should help in your process of turning around your business without alienating those that you count on and that are counting on you.

The definition of a key stakeholder is "anyone who has a stake in the success of your business." That would be both internal and external stakeholders.

Examples are:

- Employees
- Suppliers
- Vendors
- Customers
- Creditors

- Investors (if applicable)
- Board of directors (if applicable)
- and your family

Some people would even argue that the community is a stakeholder in the success of your business. What is your current situation regarding communication to any of the stakeholders mentioned? When a business is struggling, it's very natural to try to keep it as quiet as possible.

I've been there, I know exactly how it feels, and it can be a very embarrassing time. It's humiliating to admit that your company is not doing as well as you would like for it to. The point I want to make here is that lack of communication will often backfire on you and it creates more tension with your stakeholders. You see, they very likely already realize that something is not going right. The fact that you don't communicate with them can make it even worse. When a business owner fails to communicate with key stakeholders, it breeds mistrust and negative assumptions. This could cause them to take actions that will actually worsen your business situation.

Creating a Communication Plan

This communication plan will be used to share what's appropriate to each audience. The elements of your communication plan will include:

- Your current situation
- A little bit about how we got here
- What we plan to do about it
- Some idea of when we expect to see improvement

- How you plan to continue your communication with our stakeholders

Start with the what and the why. Here, you're going to explain clearly and briefly the current state and maybe a little bit about how you got here. Here's a simple example; "Sales and cash flow have dropped dramatically over the last 18 months." In this example you could further point out that, "We are getting increased pressure from a new competitor that took two of our largest clients." You might even admit that you've just not put quite enough effort into new customer acquisition. This is just an example, but it might be the type of thing you would say when you start talking about the what and the why.

Next, what are you going to do about it? Share briefly what your turnaround strategy is. An example here might be saying, "We are implementing the processes learned in the *Business Turnaround Blueprint* book and training. This training is helping us put together a strategy to improve in the areas the company needs improvement in." You might also mention some of the actions you plan on taking, such as putting pressure on collections and accounts receivable to try to help bring in more cash flow. To address one of your other issues that might have been and your first one is, "We're implementing a new marketing plan to get new customers." You could even say something like, "We've also put a halt on all overtime to help reduce cost." This again is just a simple example.

Next, you might want to communicate your expectations for the recovery. Here's another example: "We expect the marketing efforts to take about three months before we see enough results to improve revenue. We believe accounts receivable will improve in the next 30 days because of our improvement in collection practices that will help improve cash flow." You might even mention, "We'll use that improved cash flow to reduce our debts and pay our invoices on time." You could even give a little more timeframe information such as, "We expect to get through this period in the next six months." Be realistic here. It would be better here to under promise and over deliver.

Another thing you might want to communicate is your sincere apology for your past poor communication. It's very important that you exhibit optimism for the future or that you've got this and you're going to turn this situation around. Show confidence that you put together a turnaround plan that you know is going to work. And be bold and ask for their support. You might even have to ask for their patience and then express appreciation for their support. Finish up with a promise to provide much more frequent updates on your situation.

Vendor Negotiations

Your vendors would rather be paid over time than try to shut you down for non-payment. Provide your vendors with your turnaround plan and tell them what you're doing. Consider creating a repayment plan for them and show them how you expect to pay them back. For example; your repayment plan might be as simple as, for every new invoice you expect to pay 10% down on past invoices. When appropriate, you might provide financial statements but only provide this when asked. You might want to offer being put on COD (if they haven't already put you on COD) as time goes on, and then pay down the old invoices over time.

So here is what I consider some vendor musts. You've got to be consistent with your communication. Don't avoid their calls, talk to them, be proactive, and reach out to them first. When you make a commitment, keep it. You're trying to rebuild their trust. You need your vendors and you need their trust. If your plan doesn't go as you expect it to, then be quick to communicate with them any changes.

Key Employees

I realize there is the real risk of losing valuable employees during this difficult time in your business. It's important that you assure employees that your current plans will turn around the company. Again, here is a time you must show your confidence and faith in your turnaround plan. You might even consider offering them some sort of incentive to stick with you through the storm that you're in right now. Be certain that you get them involved in the process of turning around your organization. Turning around your company is a good cause that they can get behind and support. Everyone likes to fight for a good cause.

Communicating with Bankers

It is natural to be afraid to communicate with bankers because they have leverage and can call your notes. Some people believe that they should only talk to their bankers when the bankers ask for information. This is a place where I think it's important for you to be proactive. I'm sure there are exceptions but in my past personal experience, working closely with bankers during tough times was a benefit, not a negative. If you handle it properly, your bankers can actually help you during a very tough time. For example, I've had bankers put my notes on interest only for six months to help me get through a tough cash flow time. Bankers are just like your other creditors; they don't want to see you go under, they just want to be assured they will get their money back.

I recognize this is a risk but you will have to talk with your loan officers sooner or later. Trust me, you don't want your bankers find out your business is in trouble as a surprise. I think it's best to get them involved in your turnaround strategic plan. With your bankers, be sure to share your strategic turnaround plan that you've developed through the processes described in this book. I recommend that you be proactive and send them monthly financial statements. I would even go as far as to sending them graphs on your key performance indicators. Consider taking your banker to lunch quarterly and going over how things are going in your organization. I guarantee you, most bankers do not have clients that are as open and honest with them as I'm recommending you be. Invite your banker to come to your business on a regular basis and encourage them to drop by at any time to see how things are going. Show them the progress you're making and the things you're proud of. If done properly, your banker is a great strategic partner in your turnaround plan.

Another thing your banker might help you with, if needed, is an accounts receivable loan. If you have a large note, consider working with your loan officer to renegotiate terms of the loan. As I mentioned earlier I was once in this situation (a couple of times really) and I asked the banker to suspend my principal for six months. Bankers are involved in a lot of businesses and have a lot of information. Ask for their advice and suggestions on your turnaround strategy, get their input.

Taking Action

Here are some action items to take away from this chapter:

I do want to end this encouraging you to look at your current communication style and make sure that you're communicating properly to your stakeholders. I can't stress enough how damaging poor communication can be in a time like this. Don't let your key stakeholders fear the worst. Be open and honest and upfront to the degree that's possible.

- Develop a communication plan
- Review the turnaround plan with your employees and get them involved
- Communicate early and often with your creditors
- Apologize to all stakeholders that you have not communicated with properly

Chapter 6
Quality Products and Services

In this chapter, we will be focusing on the quality of your products and services and how they have impact on your turnaround. There are two common issues related to the quality of your products and services. First, it's possible that the slipping of quality of your products and services has contributed to some of the business struggles you are facing right now. Second, it's also common that in response to business challenges, you've attempted to reduce cost, which has impacted the quality of your products and services. It is critical that your business turnaround journey includes the appropriate focus on product and service quality. Letting quality slip will put your business into a death spiral that you may not be able to pull out of.

Once quality has slipped it can be very difficult to recover from, especially with your customers. What is quality?

- Quality can be described as "fitness of use"
- Quality can be a product or service that meets or exceeds customer expectations
- Quality might be that your product or service is better than your competitors

Fitness of use means your product or service does exactly what it's supposed to do from the perspective of you customer. Poor quality would mean that it doesn't do exactly what it's supposed to do.

Meeting customer expectations is simply satisfying the customer, and your product or service meets what the customer defines as quality. In this case, customer perception determines the quality of products and services. When you are exceeding customer expectation, you have wowed your customer. Has your product or service exceeded their expectations? We call this "delighting" or "wowing" the customer. Your ability to "wow" the customer can make the difference on customer retention and growing the customer base.

Quality might also be measured by how much better your product and services are as compared to your competitors'. What matters most here is how your customer perceives your quality and your quality as they compare it to your competition.

What is the quality level of your products or services? Based on these definitions that I've just gone over, what is the customer's quality perception of your products and services? You might want to ask your customers and you should also ask your employees. How do your employees feel about the quality and services they are producing?

Here's a concept that I'd like to share with you, it's called the Kano model. The basic concept of the Kano model is that what your customers once thought was exceptional will become the norm. What you must do is make an effort to stay ahead of the customers' expectations. You need to find new ways to delight your customers, and if you don't, your competitors will. Here's how the Kano model looks in a graphic form.

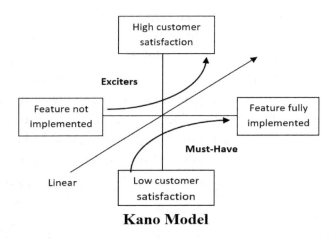

Kano Model

You can see from this chart that what once excited the customer has now become a must-have. A good example is the smartphone. Every few months a new feature comes out that becomes a must-have. What used to excite you in a feature becomes the norm. The phone industry is always trying to stay ahead of this curve and add new features that will excite you, that will of course eventually, in a few months, become a must-have for you and no longer impress you.

Philip Crosby was a pioneer in the quality industry. He authored many books including *Quality is Free, Quality without Tears, Let's Talk Quality,* and *Leading: The Art of Becoming an Executive,* among others. Crosby came up with what he called the 14 Laws. Let me go over them quickly here. To have a quality organization, an organization that produces quality products and services, you have to have these things, in his mind.

1. Management Commitment
2. Quality Improvement Teams
3. Measure Processes
4. Cost of Quality
5. Quality Awareness
6. Correct Problems
7. Monitor Progress
8. Train Supervisors
9. Zero Defects Day
10. Establish Improvement Goals
11. Remove Fear
12. Recognize
13. Quality Councils
14. Repeat the Cycle

First you have to have a management commitment. It all starts at the top.

He believed in creating quality improvement teams. It was very important in his mind that you measure all your processes.

He coined the term, "Cost of quality." It was very important to him that you know exactly what quality costs or what the lack of quality costs your organization.

He wanted the whole employee base to have a full quality awareness. It was very important that you have a process to correct problems. It was very important to him that you monitor your progress. He felt that supervisors should be trained in quality.

Crosby instituted a concept called "Zero Defects Day."

It was very important to establish improvement goals in your organization.

He really believed that organizational leaders had to remove the fear. If you don't remove fear of the process, you'll have employees hiding quality issues. Don't allow your environment to get to the point where employees can't point out quality issues to you as an owner.

He felt it was very important that you create an environment where you recognize quality and recognize employees for helping you improve quality.

He created what was called Quality Councils, where you'd have a group of leaders in your organization that would review quality metrics on a regular basis.

And then the last, the 14th one, was that you must keep repeating the cycle. Review all of the 13 previous steps and make sure you keep this process going. Crosby's 14 Laws is a very good place to start as you try to work on improving the quality of your products and services.

I mentioned that Crosby came up with the term "cost of quality." It's very important that you understand the real cost of having poor quality. If you lose customers over quality, the lifetime value of those customers could have a very large financial impact to your company. If you have to inspect quality into your process, that is a very expensive process. You should look at returns and refunds as part of your cost of poor quality. You also need to consider lost opportunity costs. If you're spending a lot of time and resources on fixing things, then you are losing opportunity for increased sales, profits, and customers.

And lastly, reputation costs. Once you have a reputation of poor quality in the community or in the eyes of your customers, it's very difficult to regain it. The cost of poor quality is very much like an iceberg.

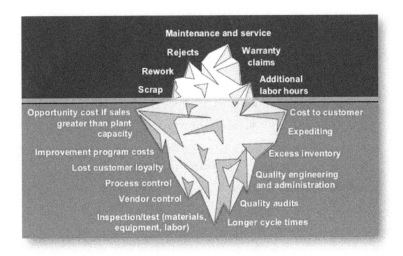

You have a few things at the top that are easy to spot, such as maintenance, rejects, reworks, scrap, additional labor, warranty claims, those kinds of things.

Those are just the tip of the iceberg. Below the iceberg, you have a lot of other things that you likely don't look at as or realize is a cost of poor quality. Other cost of poor quality to consider are: expediting costs, excess inventory, quality engineering, quality audits, cycle times, inspection of materials, labor, equipment, vendor control, process control, lost customer loyalty, improvement program costs, opportunity cost of lost sales. All these things and many more you may uncover in your organization are below the surface, but they all add to the cost of poor quality in the organization. It's estimated that poor quality cost for a typical company can be 15% to 20% of annual sales. You don't see this line on your balance sheet, but it's there, hidden in all of your other operational costs.

I want to talk now about the impact of appearance, because appearance can impact your customer's perception of quality. For example, your employees' attire and their demeanor can have effect on your customers' perception. The look of your office and facilities, your packaging, the look of your website, your quotations, invoices, business cards, brochures, etc. All of these things can have an impact on how your customer perceives the quality of your products and services. As a business owner, you have to keep your eye on everything. Don't let yourself get so close to your business that you can't see some of these things from the customers' perspective.

Customer Service

It's very important for you to analyze the quality of your customer service, which will impact customer-perceived quality. Start off by asking your customers how they feel and what would make quality better in their perception. I think it's very wise as a business owner to monitor from time to time the phone calls or other interactions that your customers have with your employees. I've heard of business owners who have placed orders with their own company, had them shipped to their home, just to see how it looks and how it appears from a customer's perspective. It is very important that you train your employees in exceptional customer service skills.

Here's just a short list of things you want to make sure you implement:

- Make sure your employees are patient with your customers
- Train them to be good listeners
- Your employees must know how to give clear and positive communication with your customers
- I'm sure you recognize that it's very important that your customer service people, people that are on the frontline talking to your customers, need to have a good basic knowledge of your products and services, maybe not all the technical aspects of them, but they should have a good understanding of what you offer your customers.
- Make sure your employees are cool under pressure. Of course, every once in a while, you'll get that irate customer that just wants to blow off steam. Your employees need to know how to keep their cool when things get hot. Teach your employees how to be persuasive, how they can influence the customer in a positive way.

Here I want to go over what I see are some common customer service mistakes that can really hurt your organization. The first is just putting the wrong employees in a position where they interact closely with customers. The wrong employee with the wrong attitude can drastically hurt your customer relationships.

A common mistake is not putting enough training into customer contact employees, teaching them the customer service skills and requirements that I mentioned earlier. Another mistake is not monitoring customer service, making sure as an owner you know exactly how customer service is going in your organization. Another mistake I see is not taking action quickly to correct issues and letting things slide way too long. It may mean removing an employee from a position even though you need somebody there, but it's critical that you take action on what you know you need to do when it comes to customer service.

A common mistake business owners make is putting untrained, negative, lethargic and unprofessional-looking employees with no people skills in a high customer contact position. Owners feel they are saving money but in the end, it's very costly. A good example I've seen of this in the past is putting the lowest skilled, lowest paid person in a delivery position. Sometimes the delivery person is the only contact customers have with the organization. You need to make sure that the employees that have the most contact with your customers are the ones who you invest in and make sure they're paid well, they look nice, and they know how to present themselves well, because they're representing you and your company.

How about starting a quality initiative in your company? The quality improvement is going to start with you. Communicate clearly with your employees what your quality goals are. Establish some quality metrics with your employees, so you can show them how quality is improving, or decreasing, for that matter. Some metrics examples I've used in the past year are things like:

- How many returns are coming in each week or each month?
- How many customer complaint calls are coming in and how well are they being handled?
- We've already mentioned cost of quality, creating some metrics around how much money is being spent on quality inspection.

These are the types of metrics I'm talking about here. Then, recognize and reward for quality. When you do see improvement in quality metrics, throw a party. Find some way to recognize and reward those who are improving the quality of your products and services.

Invest in training your employees. You've got to train your employees in quality. Training is the place to start to get your employees involved in the quality improvement effort. Teach them the Six Sigma Problem-Solving Process. This is something I'll go into more detail later. Teach them how to work together in problem-solving teams. Help them understand the impact and the cost of poor quality.

Taking Action

Here are some action items to take away from this chapter:

- Determine your customers' perception of the quality of your products and services.

- Find out what your customers really think. This may really surprise you, may be an eye-opening experience.

- Train your employees in quality improvement tools.

- Create quality metrics. Work with your employees to figure out how you can measure the quality as it improves over time.

- Make quality a part of your overall business culture and train every employee that comes in contact with a customer in customer service skills.

Chapter 7
Customers - Getting Them and Keeping Them

One of the big mistakes I see business owners make, and that I was also guilty of, is to cut back on marketing costs and efforts when times get tough. Of course, you should drop all marketing efforts that are not giving you a good return on your investment. Now is the time to aggressively find new clients. Sales has a way of overcoming many past business mistakes. In this chapter, I will cover customer acquisition, your marketing channels, marketing and direct response marketing, your unique selling proposition, the lead generation funnel, referrals, your sales team, and customer satisfaction.

As an overview, I want to start off explaining that each area discussed in this chapter barely hits the highlights. There's so much more to learn about marketing, customer acquisition, getting them and keeping them. This chapter is simply an attempt to steer you in the right direction and to help you look at what you might need to be working on to improve your customer acquisition process. I want you to start thinking about increasing your marketing efforts. As we look at these various subjects, find an area that best fits you, your industry, and the customer base that you focus on. Be sure to get help in the area that you're weak or where you don't have the adequate resources on staff. This is all about developing a marketing plan.

Customer Acquisition

I believe finding and keeping new customers is an essential piece of your business turnaround strategy. But it's very important that you make sure new customers are at profitable margins, have the ability to pay, and pay promptly. If your new customers don't fit these three categories, you can very easily get yourself in even deeper trouble.

Here's a graphic I found very valuable. It compares what advertising looked like in the 1980s to what advertising looks like today.

There are so many more marketing channels. Certainly, social media and internet-based marketing has really changed the whole landscape of channels that you can effectively use to promote your business.

It makes the decision on how to best market your business tougher than ever. You have to figure out the best marketing channel for your business and for the clientele you're going after. How do you pick the right marketing channel? Well, the right channel for your customer is the one that your customer is using. To find that, you need to know your customers, you need to know their demographics and their psychographics. Demographics are things such as the country they live in, the city, their age, gender, these kinds of things. Psychographics is more like the kinds of things they might read, shows they may watch or their overall attitude about life in general, and philosophy. These and many more would fit in the psychographic category.

One tool to help you pick the right channel is to simply to ask your current clients what media they pay attention to. While I try not to overly worry about what my competitors are doing in marketing, at least learn the channels they are using. They may have found a media channel that works best in your industry. So, check out how your competitors are marketing their products and services. This may be a case where you need to get some help from marketing experts, people that can help you determine the very best way to market to your potential clients.

The biggest marketing mistake business owners make, and this one I've made many times myself, so I'm not saying I'm above this, but the biggest mistake business owners make is inconsistent marketing.

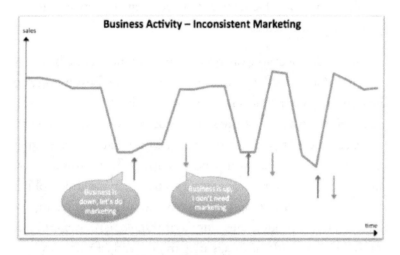

This graphic is a really good example of showing how people will only market when business is down. When business is good, they don't feel like they need to market. When business is bad, they jump out there and think they have to market. But I've also seen it go the other way. When business is bad, they pull all their funds back and not market at all. The real mistake here is simply being inconsistent. You need a very consistent marketing process no matter how things are going in your business.

There are really two major types of marketing. One fits in the category called "Mass Marketing." This is really about brand awareness. This is best for the big companies like Coke and Nike and Apple. The really big brands, they can just focus on mass marketing and brand awareness. The average business owner should focus on "Direct Response Marketing." This is to evoke immediate response, something that you can measure, such as a phone call or maybe a visit to your website.

Direct Response Marketing

If you place some sort of a direct response marketing ad, it would have these characteristics: First, it would be trackable, you'd be able to know where that lead source came from. It would be measurable, you'd be able to measure how many leads you got from that ad. It would have compelling headlines and copy, something that really draws attention to your product or service and it would target a very specific niche. It wouldn't be broad. It would be very focused on a particular niche in your industry. And you would make a very specific offer and it would be an offer that demands a response. You might make it time-based so that your client would have to act by a certain date to get a certain discount. That would be an example of a demand response. Then your marketing would have a follow-up system. As leads come into the system, you'd have a way of following up on them.

There are a couple approaches you could take when it comes to direct response. You could have a one-shot approach. This is where you're really going after an immediate sale. But probably what's more effective is what's called a campaign approach. This is where you're out there capturing leads and then you have a follow-up sequence. It'd be multiple emails, multiple mailings, and then in each case you end with making an offer.

Content marketing is another approach to consider. This is a strategic marketing approach that's focused on creating and distributing valuable, relevant, and consistent content to attract and retain highly qualified leads. The formats for this include things like blog posts, producing videos, even material like eBooks and white papers. These are all good examples of content marketing.

Here's an example of mass marketing with a branding example. This is an image from one of my other training programs called "Business For Sale Blueprint."

If I were to do a billboard for this product and all I showed was my logo, that would be simply branding, just trying to make the customers aware of the product or service name.

But a direct response example for the same billboard would be to at least add a phone number so I could track how many responses I get from that billboard. Even a better direct response would be to show more about what the product or services and have some sort of call to action, "Call now to save 20%," something like that. But at least having some way to track the responses, at the least, is required in a direct response approach.

Unique Selling Proposition (USP)

The USP is very important and so often overlooked by many business owners. Most business owners don't really understand the concept of their unique selling proposition. Your company's USP is all about the position you want and the image of your business you want to hold in the mind of your potential clients as compared to your competitors. What sets your company apart, your product and service? What makes it different? And, why should a prospective client choose your product or service over the competition?

Here's a little advice on creating your USP. Step number one is to describe your target audience. Examples might be soccer moms between the ages of 35 and 42 that live in a particular city, in a particular neighborhood, and have a particular income. Know your target audience. Step number two is to explain the problem you solve. Be able to articulate exactly what you offer to your clients and what problem it will solve. Now list your biggest distinctive benefits. Clearly define your promise. Now that you've got that down, combine it, rework it. Come up with a phrase that best describes your USP. Continue to cut it down until you have as few words as possible but still gets the point across to your customers what it is that you're all about. I recommend you go through this exercise with your employees. Have them help you come up with what your USP is for your organization. This will help you and your marketing. It will also help your employees to better understand what your business and your products and services are all about.

Knowing Your Target Customer

How well do you know your customers? Again, what are their demographics and what are their psychographics? What is their biggest pain point? What would it take to motivate them to buy your product or service? Where do they hang out? What do they read? What are their hobbies? What kind of age range are they? What's their gender? What's their marital status? What's their education and their income? How big of an organization you want to market to? This is just a small portion of the questions you might ask yourself about your potential clients.

Be sure to do a thorough job of knowing exactly who your target client customer is.

So some other help for you in defining your target market is to look at your current customer base. Really analyze your current customers and see what you can find out about them and their demographics and psychographics. Check out your competition. Who are they marketing to? Do they have a better USP or do they have a better way of describing who they're after as a target client? You can also look more carefully at your products and services. Who do they best fit? Now choose a specific demographic to target and then consider the psychographics of your target. Now evaluate your decision.

Sales 101

What I call **Sales 101** is the high-level process that you go through to acquire a new customer. First, you have to qualify the customer. Make sure they really have a need for your products and services. Then you must build trust. Next, educate the customer about your products and services, and then you close the sale. At a very high level, this is a process that you're going to go through with every new client.

Customer Qualification

To qualify a customer, you have to make sure that they have a clear need or desire for what your product and service offers. You must make sure they can afford your product or service. You want to be working with people that actually have the authority to purchase your product or service. And the timing has to be right for them to purchase your product or service. An example of timing might be a business who cannot purchase in the current fiscal year or till a certain budget cycle comes around. That would at least be a potential customer that's not qualified to purchase now.

Building Trust

Clients simply don't want to buy from businesses that they don't know, like, or trust. Your job is to build up that trust, help them to know you, your products or services, and to like you. Next comes customer education, and this will go a long way toward helping them know, like, and trust you. This is where you make sure your customers know the features and benefits of your products and services. You are helping them learn more about your business and your unique selling proposition. I don't want to take too much of your time about customer education. There are a lot of good books and training on this subject and I can't do it justice here. Realize the importance of building trust and search for the tools and training that will help you build up that trust in the eyes of your prospect.

Closing the Sale

A person in sales has to be prepared to close the sale. There is very good training on this subject but be careful of formulas and canned closes. Your potential client will spot a cheesy closing trick and run for the hills. Throughout the process, you may offer several trial closes. You may use an assumptive close where throughout the whole process, your demeanor and your language shows that you just assume they're going to want to buy your product or service. And you want to make sure that when you do close, it's a very pressure-free closing question and then you just have to be quiet. Let them respond first. Depending on their response, then you decide the next step. But by all means, stay away from high-pressure closing. That doesn't work in this day and age the way it did in the past. You need to develop a very low-pressure closing style.

I like the approach of one trainer that said they don't believe in closing. His approach was to address every potential objection to buying his product during the presentation. Instead of having to use closing tricks his clients were already sold and would interrupt the presentation to say "where do I sign?" Now that should be your goal also. This starts with knowing your customer and what their likely objections are. Already have in mind your best answer to handle their likely concerns. In the end, many sales are lost simply because you didn't ask for the sale.

Lead Generation Funnel

I am a big believer that you need a lead generation funnel. The process of the funnel is to first educate your prospect on what you offer, then you create a relationship of trust, you make them an offer, and then you close the sale. Here's what a lead generation funnel looks like. You move every prospect through a funnel process of awareness, interest/consideration, intent/desire, action/purchase, and then you work on building loyalty and turning clients into advocates.

Be sure that everyone in sales in your organization understands the funnel process. Here's a simple example of a lead generation funnel.

- A potential client responds to a marketing piece
- They are put on a mailing list and sent a brochure

- A sales rep is assigned to follow up on that lead, that lead is qualified then as a prospect
- The sales rep continues to work with that prospect and shows them the value proposition of your product and service
- Then, over time, that lead becomes a client

Now, this is an example using a sales force, but you can also do a lead generation funnel that may be all direct mail or phone marketing. Each business will develop their own lead generation funnel and system.

Referral System

Another thing you need to have in your marketing arsenal is a referral system. To have an effective referral system, you have to know exactly who your target customer is, as mentioned earlier. Then you educate anyone that might refer you to what your target customer looks like. Then, of course, you have to ask for referrals. Be sure to recognize and show your appreciation for anyone that refers a prospect to you. Then create a measurement for your referral system for your return on investment and effectiveness. This might be another category where you could get some expert help developing an effective referral system in your organization.

An expert in building referral systems is Jay Abraham. I bought his program years ago titled "Jay Abraham's 93 Referral Systems" and it opened my eyes to the many ways a person could go about getting referrals. One of my favorites goes something like this: A salesman sits down with a potential client to give a presentation and somewhere in the presentation he makes this bold statement. "Bob, I just want to let you know that my business is different from most. You see, I don't spend any money on marketing and get all my business from referrals. This allows me to keep my costs down and provide better value to my clients. I need to let you know that should you decide to do business with me, I will need you to provide me with 3 to 5 people you feel I can help just the way I have helped you. Of course, this is only if you are extremely satisfied with my services. Bob, can I get your commitment that you will help me with this?" Anyway, this is how I remember it. You get the idea. Check out his program and make sure you put one or more referral mechanisms in place. I am sure you are aware that a referral is the best possible prospect.

Sales Force

If you're the type of organization that has a sales team, you must be able to measure their performance. What are your sales metrics? Are they really salespeople or are they simply order takers? Do you have a process for monitoring their activity? Do you know what really motivates your sales force?

I've always liked the analogy that running a sales force is like herding cats (salespeople may not find that so funny). Often, you'll find that salespeople march to the beat of a different drummer. You must create a motivation system that works for their personality type.

One of my pet peeves on sales teams is the lack of measurement I find missing in most of the organizations I have worked with. Often business owners don't have a clue how effective their sales team actually is. The two metrics that must be watched is are they bringing in new clients and are these clients profitable. I will commonly see situations where sales people were handed some house clients years ago and have made no effort to go out and find additional clients. This is not a sales person, this is simply a glorified order taker or customer service rep. If they are not bringing in new customers, call them what they really are and pay them accordingly.

Customer List

Here is a way of increasing sales that I find often overlooked by many businesses. You could potentially have a huge increase in sales just by mining your old customer list. Make sure you keep your customer database current. Call and check in with your past customers at least twice a year. This also helps keep your database updated. Simply send them a letter now and then remind them you appreciate your past business and would like to help them again when the need arises. Sending a monthly newsletter is a great tool to keep them informed in a very non-intrusive non-salesy way. There are many businesses that swear by this strategy as one of their most effective marketing tools.

Be sure to send them information about new developments of products and services. Just stay in touch on a regular basis with past customers. I once worked with a client who had 20 years of past installations that they had done, very large projects, and he'd never kept in touch with them at all.

Many businesses will find as they start touching base with old customers that they can increase their sales quickly and renew those relationships.

Customer Acquisition Cost

I think it's part of any good sales program that you know exactly what it costs you to acquire a new customer. Knowing this number can drive your promotions and sales strategy. Here's a simple example. Look at your P&L and see how much you spent in annual sales and marketing costs. For this example, we will use $240,000. Then go look at the year and find out how many new customers you acquired that year. This example has 73 new customers. When you do the math, you find out that each new customer actually costs you over $3,000. Now if your average customer spends $10,000 or $50,000, that may be okay, but if your average sale is only a $1,000 or $2,000, you lost money. I may have oversimplified the calculations required to determine customer acquisition costs but the point is you need to know what it costs you to acquire a new customer.

Customer Lifetime Value

Here's a simple formula for determining customer lifetime value which is also important to know when considering what you are willing to pay to acquire a customer. You take the average customer sale, the average gross profit percentage per sale, the average sales per year per customer, and the average length of time a customer is expected to stay with you.

Formula:

A - Average customer sale

B - Average sale gross profit percentage

C - Average sales per year per customer

D - Average length of time customer stays with you

$$CLV = A \times B \times C \times D$$

Your customer lifetime value equals A times B times C times D. Let's give you a real-life example

Example:

- Average Sale: $2,000

- Average Gross Profit: 30%

- Average GP per sale: $600

- Average Sales per Year: 1

- Average Annual Sales: $2,000

- Average Years Customer: 5.5

- Average CLV: $11,000

- Average CLV Gross Profit: $3,300

Let's just say your average sale is $2,000. Your average gross profit is 30% with an average gross profit per sale of $600. But you're only going to make one sale per year on average to this client. The average annual sale per new client would be $2,000. Now let's just say you keep that customer on average 5.5 years. From a sales point of view, your customer lifetime value would be $11,000. And over the life of that customer, you would make a gross profit of approximately $3,300.

Now that you know that number, you can have a better idea from a marketing point of view of how much you could afford to spend to acquire that new customer. Obviously, it would need to be way below $3,000.

Sales Metrics

A ratio I'd like to recommend here is a customer-win ratio. I think it's very important that you have this sales metric in your arsenal. For every proposal or quote that you give, what percentage of them do you win? Knowing this win ratio will help you make decisions about your sales and bidding processes. It's amazing to me how many sales people and business owners don't know this win ratio. It's a very important metric. Go back as soon as possible and determine what your customer-win ratio is.

How about your sales call performance? It's very important to have a sales metric for direct sales people to measure their sales call effectiveness. Now, the truth is, sales people, by nature, do not like to track performance metrics. If you pay any type of base or offer benefits, they should provide a minimum amount of performance information. Now, I would make an exception for commission-only sales reps but I would teach them the value of measuring this kind of performance metric. I wouldn't require them to share it since I'm paying them for the results they provide.

Customer Satisfaction

I think it's very important that you know your customer satisfaction level. This is really the first step in keeping your customers.

A great place to start is with employee satisfaction. If you have unhappy employees that are disgruntled, it's going to be very hard to keep your customers happy. It's important that you show customers how much they're appreciated, that they're not taken for granted. I like to use a survey to track customer satisfaction levels. Another tool is to hold customer focus groups where you bring them in, maybe even with a third party, to get information about how they feel as a customer and how you can better serve them.

Customer Retention

Here are just a few keys to customer retention:

- Frequent communication. It's very hard to over-communicate with your customers.

- Make sure their experience is consistent. They need to know the level of service they can expect every time. If you wow them one time and then abuse them the next, they're not going to stay with you.

- Try to exceed expectations at every opportunity.

- Try to build dependency. Try to give a service level that makes your clients dependent on you and have no desire to find another provider.

- Implement a complaint management system. Be sure you make it easy for customers to complain and know that you will take action on their complaints.

- Implement a "wow" factor. At every opportunity, wow your customers. It's not that hard to do.

Taking Action

Here are some action items to take away from this chapter:

- Develop your USP (get your employees and come up with your own unique selling proposition)
- Make sure that you're implementing a direct response marketing approach
- Determine your customer acquisition costs
- Determine the lifetime value of your customers
- Develop your sales performance metrics and evaluate your sales team if you have one.

Finding customers and keeping them is a very important tool in your turnaround strategy.

Chapter 8
Getting Employees Involved

In this chapter, we are discussing getting your employees involved in the turnaround of your business. You see, your employees have a huge stake in you improving your business. Their jobs are at stake, their livelihoods, and their families are involved. They're a huge stakeholder. So many of us business owners try to hide our problems from our employees, but we need to get them involved to make the changes necessary to improve your business. You see, your employees could be your biggest asset in turning around your business. You must properly harness their creativity and create an environment of trust. Don't overlook this valuable resource in your turnaround efforts.

Employees as an Asset

Here are some important questions about employees you must ask yourself;

- Do you recognize the fact that your employees are a very valuable asset?
- How do you really view your employees?

- Do you look at them as an asset or do deep down you really feel having employees is just a necessary evil of doing business?
- Do your employees really know that you value them?
- What do they sense about your attitudes towards them as employees?
- Have you solicited their help at all in turning around your business?

In this chapter, I'm trying to make the case of how important it is to get your employees involved. Have you just tried to keep some of the struggles of your business to yourself? Whether you want to admit it or not, your employees know you're having challenges, you can't hide that from employees. They may not know the exact details but they can read the situation better than you realize. No matter how close you've kept your challenges to the vest, your employees know what's going on in your company.

Leadership Speech

I recommend you gather all your employees together and give them the "failure-is-not-an-option" speech. You should share with them the challenges that you're facing in your company. Lay it all out on the table. You may not share every minor detail that you're dealing with, but you do want to let them know that your company is in trouble, that you're having some difficulties, and that you need their support. You should also tell your employees what you're doing about it. Tell them you are working through these *Business Turnaround Blueprint*™ principles and strategies that will help turnaround your company. And then ask for their help. Again, as mentioned before, they're very vested in helping you turn around the business.

Purge

This section may seem a little harsh, but I suggest you ask employees to leave immediately if they do not buy in to helping you turn around your company. The last thing you need is a few employees throwing stones at your plans while they are still within the organization. Offer to call it a layoff, but you don't want them around in a turnaround effort if they are not fully on board. Next, you should give every employee notice that any lack of support that you see in the future will be grounds for immediate termination. You only want people with you that support your efforts and are there to fight with you to save and turn around your company. As I've mentioned, non-supportive employees will only bring down the company and they're going to sabotage your chances for success.

Again, it may be harsh, but you really must remove those people that are going to hurt your chances of survival. I've seen many companies fail to take this step. They'll say something like, "Well, in 20 years, we've never had a layoff and I'm not going to start now." I would argue that saving your business, saving the jobs of those who really want to be a part of your company is the most important thing. If you have to let a few people go that really don't want to be a part of that plan, then that's a necessary evil. We're talking about saving your company. We're talking about increasing the profitability of your company and making your company more valuable to you and your employees. Remove employees that are not on the bus and aren't with you (*Good to Great* metaphor).

Motivation

It is also important that you understand what motivates employees. You see, each employee has their own personality style, their own personality profile. In today's modern management, you can't treat every employee the same, you have to recognize the differences between employees. I like a very economical assessment tool called the DISC profile. This is something you can take and get a better understanding of each employee's different communication style. In this profile, there's no right or wrong, but it helps each employee understand how they can best communicate with each other. The DISC profile also helps you as a manager know what works best in communicating with each employee.

And I'll talk about a little bit later, but you need to know the differences in generational motivation. Of course, there are exceptions, but we'll talk about that in a moment. I highly recommend that you promise some sort of future reward, even if you can't clearly articulate what it's going to be, tell your employees that for those who stick with you, you will make it right for them. And be sure that you stick with that.

Train

Many of us owners and leaders fail when it comes to properly training our employees. Here's where you can really help your employees know what they can do to help in the turnaround of your business. I recommend you work on teaching your employees some team-building skills. There's a lot of great training and materials out there on that, so look for some ways to build the team up. Maybe even do some events together that are good team-building exercises.

Work on teaching your employees strong problem-solving skills. Of course, me being involved in Lean Six Sigma, I like the DMAIC Problem-Solving Process, which I'll share more on later in this book. It's also important that you focus on teaching employee's high-level customer service skills. Don't let a downturn in your business affect the way your employees treat your customers. It's very important that your customers get excellent service during this time. Be sure you keep your employees current on technical skill requirements. If your cash flow doesn't allow you to hire some outside training, then start an in-house training program. A low-cost training solution is to have your employees read a book together and teach each other what they learned from the book and how it could be applied to your business. Don't let money get in the way of keeping up the training of your employees.

Measure

In this book I talk a lot about measuring things, and here's another great place to measure. Of course you have to inspect what you expect, so be sure to track your employees' performance wherever possible. I highly recommend the practice of MBWA, Management By Walking Around. You've probably heard of this before. We too often sit in our offices, working on problems and challenges and don't get out and get a real feel, a real vibe of what it's like, what the morale is in our company, and how things are going. Also get involved in quality issues and customer relation issues. Get out there and spend some time with your employees every day. I don't care what high-level position you are in your organization, get out there and spend some time with your employees.

Share daily, weekly and monthly metrics. Let your employees know how things are going. Tell them how sales are improving or not improving. Share the areas of the business that still need work. Tell them about some big wins, maybe some failures, but keep your employees informed and celebrate even the small successes. Celebrate immediately and often. Bring in some pizza and say "Hey, we accomplished XYZ!" Keep the morale up in your employees. Help them understand they're a part of something and they're making a difference in your organization. Learn some low-cost employee motivation strategies. There are some great books out there like *101 Ways to Motivate Employees for $10 or Less,* or any similar title. Learn how you can motivate your employees without spending a lot of money.

Firm but Fair

Being "firm but fair" might be a challenge for you if you've had a history of tolerating poor performance. It depends on what your management style has been, but I've seen a lot of companies that have let poor performance go on year after year after year and they've let it get to a point where it's very hard to go back in and do anything about it. Now, it's more important than any time in the history of your company to not accept poor performance. I'm not saying that poor performers have to be cut immediately, but you must plan on how to get them up to the performance level that's required. If they don't perform at a level that's expected, then you may have to remove them from the organization. As I like to call it, you will put them into the company's Alumni Program.

Somewhere along the way, maybe even a trusted, valued employee that may have gotten a little bit of an entitlement mentality is going to challenge your resolve. Be ready for that, expect it and be ready to hit it head on. You may have to let somebody like that go if they're disrupting the turnaround of your business. Again, it's all about your business; a single individual is not worth letting your company go down because they don't want to make the changes necessary to help your company. Any employee that blatantly disregards your current situation should be dealt with firmly and swiftly. Don't let the day end without you having dealt with the problem. Of course, when it comes to dealing with and terminating employees, be sure you're following all the state and federal employee laws and regulations.

Now is a really good time to update your employee manual. Make it clear in your employee guidelines what's expected of each employee. Along those same lines, you might want to update your job descriptions and make sure your employees know clearly what is expected of them.

This is all basic stuff and I'm sure you're doing a lot of this, but I just want to remind you at this time. I like this quote from Gallup, *"The most highly motivated and productive employees push hard because they feel like their work will make a difference to obtaining worthy goals."* That's a perfect quote for your current situation. Get your employees involved, let them help you push hard because they know they're saving the business, they're helping you make a difference. Make sure that your employees feel that turning around and helping you make a success out of your company is a goal worth attaining.

Taking Action

Here are some action items to take away from this chapter:

- Do a self-examination of what your real attitude about your employees is. If it's not the right one, you'd better work on that.

- Prepare and give that rally speech I talked about.

- Gather your employees up, tell them what's going on; tell them how much you need their help to turn around your business.

- Be sure to get rid of anyone who doesn't want to be in the boat with you. If you don't get them out of the boat, they'll sink it, I guarantee you.

- Look into what training is needed in your organization and put together some sort of training plan. And as I mentioned earlier, it doesn't have to be a costly training program. You can do this very economically.

- Look at how you're going to measure performance and how you're going to let your employees know that they're making a difference in the turnaround of your company.

- Update that employee manual, but enforce it and enforce it fairly.

In this chapter, I'm simply highlighting the fact that you need to be working on this stuff. You need to get your employees involved. Stop thinking you're hiding your challenges from your employees, you're not. Get them involved and have them help you turn around your company. Again, they're your greatest asset in your organization. They are the ones that are meeting the needs of your customers. Without your employees you cannot service the needs of your customers.

Chapter 9
Key Business Metrics

In this chapter, we're going to be talking a little bit more about metrics. I have mentioned metrics before, but we'll go in to a lot more depth in this chapter. I believe that when business owners systematically measure and track all their key business metrics, they will take control of their own destiny. Failure to track them and make the needed rapid adjustments leads to uncontrolled chaos and of course frustration.

Answer the following questions:

- How does your company compare with your industry?
- Do you know how your company compares with competitors?
- Tell me how your company compares with your own past results?
- Do you have enough metrics to show whether you're improving or going down?
- Now tell me how does your company capture and monitor your metrics?

The truth is, most business owners I consult with can't effectively answer these questions. That's what this chapters all about, how do you get there? How do we get to where we can answer these questions properly?

Key Performance Indicators

Let's talk about Key Performance Indicators, or KPIs for short. First, they must reflect your company's goals. You need KPIs that point you to what the company wants to accomplish this week, this month, this year and then beyond. KPIs are high level and the key to your company's success. KPIs must be quantifiable. If you can't measure it, of course you will not be able to track it and it wouldn't be a metric. Here are some typical KPI categories:

- Sales and Marketing
- Human Resources
- Employee Development
- Financial
- Health and Safety
- Environmental
- Manufacturing and Operations
- Social or Community

And we'll go in to more detail about these later and give you some examples.

First, you need to select three to eight (eight is on the high side) KPIs from each of the categories that apply to your business. You might be able to pick a lot more than that, but you need to narrow it down. Get to the key, the real high-level ones that you want to watch regularly to effectively manage your business. You can't track everything, keep it high level. If possible, and you have the data, look back at the last three years of history for each metric so you can see the trends. Also, if you have some historic data in hand, now you could establish some new goals that are based on improving from the past results. I also highly recommend that you benchmark with some of the top companies in your industry, especially if you have an industry that tracks a lot of metrics that you have access to. You should look at how you compare with the top 25% in your industry and even set goals to be in the top 10%.

At a minimum, track your metrics on a monthly basis, some metrics might lend themselves to daily and weekly. I have found it very effective to post your KPIs in each department. Make sure your employees see them. Go a step further and show your metrics in your monthly employee meetings. Whenever you communicate with your employees, make sure they see the performance of your organization, especially these KPIs. Consider creating incentive plans that are related to KPIs. This could get complicated, but it's very important that employees know how important meeting the KPIs are for the success of your company. I also recommend that you find a way to link some of the KPIs to your employee performance reviews. Linking KPIs to performance reviews causes your employees to take them much more seriously.

KPI Sources

As mentioned earlier, if you're in an industry you can compare with, you might want to look at some industry standards. Many industries have associations that you can belong to that provide some of the industry standards or industry comparisons. If you can find a trade association you can join, you can get a lot of good data and comparisons of how your peers are doing in that association. Sometimes it's worth the association dues just to get your hands on this comparison data.

Your banker might also be a good source of getting information. They have access to a lot of data that help them rate companies. Your banker can show you some of the key performance indicators and metrics that they look at as they look at your company and what's important to them. Take advantage of that if it's at all possible.

Certain industries have reports that are available. They can give you an indication of some metrics that would be very valuable for you. Stay up with what's going on in your industry as much as possible. I also highly recommend joining some peer groups, either industry-related peer groups or you could have multi-industry peer groups that share information, which can help you develop KPIs in your company.

Benchmarking Process

The benchmarking process starts with clearly defining what processes, metrics or procedures you want to benchmark. Let me give you an example. Let's say you're trying to determine what would be the right "on time delivery" metric for your organization and how you might benchmark with other organizations, either in your industry or outside your industry. That would be a clearly defined process that you want to benchmark. Now, you have to look at, where might I find these benchmarking partners, where might I get data that could help me with that metric? Look at the sources we just talked about for benchmarking opportunities, but you might also look for other sources.

Here is an example from my past when I was working with a company to help them win the Malcolm Baldrige National Quality Award. One of the things that I wanted to benchmark was a good employee satisfaction metric. There are very few people in our industry that had a metric like that, so I had to look outside. I looked at the employee satisfaction of FedEx. I also found the employee satisfaction metrics for Southwest Airlines. I ended up building a chart that showed our employee satisfaction along with that of our benchmark comparisons. We also set our goals for that metric based on those benchmarks and found a way to get an annual update on their metrics.

Once you find a benchmarking partner, you must identify ways that you can collect the data and share your data with them on a scheduled basis. If your benchmark sharing partner is in another city, another state, or maybe even another industry, you must work out a way to collect data and share your data with them as they share their data with you. Now collect data from your benchmark partner and then, if possible, visit and get a real deep understanding of how their processes work and how they may be different than you. Be certain you are comparing apples for apples. In my example, when I was comparing employee satisfaction metrics, I needed to be sure their measure of 86% satisfaction meant the same as it would with our satisfaction survey methodology.

Next, determine the gap between your current results and what is "Best in Class." Sometimes when it comes to benchmarking, you have to be creative, but if at all possible, create benchmarks that compare your company with the best in your industry. Now that you see a gap in where you are and where you ought to be or would like to be, determine why that is, and set goals for future performance. Figure out how you might move the needle and get closer toward eliminating that gap and meeting those goals. Be sure to communicate these goals to all your employees and review your results regularly. You have to make this a systematic process or your efforts will really be wasted. You should follow some sort of process improvement methodology (like DMAIC or PDCA) that'll help move you to the desired goals.

As I mentioned earlier, teach your new employees the DMAIC Problem-Solving Process, getting your company involved in Baldrige, ISO, Lean, Six Sigma, each of those have process improvement methodologies that will help you reach your desired goals.

Real Life Metric Example

I'd like to share with you here an example from one of my clients that had a very large warehouse. Their employees received what were called "pull and pick orders" and they pulled these items from inventory, boxed them, and shipped them out. They had no metrics and no way of measuring performance. The warehouse crew was also failing to keep the warehouse organized and clean, so something had to be done. The business hired me to come in and create a solution. They had good records of how many pick and pulls had been daily for years. All I needed was the picks per day and the number of employee hours worked each day to create a new metric for them called "picks per man hour."

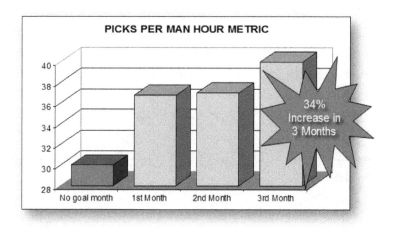

As you can see from this chart, their performance increase was 34% in just three months. This increase is simply from establishing some metrics and some goals for them to shoot at.

This is a great reminder for you that you really must give your employees a target to shoot for. A great analogy is a basketball game. Who would even watch basketball if they were just dribbling the ball around, they didn't have a goal to shoot at, and nobody kept score. Our employees need to know the score and you need to help them with that. Here, I want to provide some sample KPIs for you that you might want to consider as you decide which ones might be best in representing how you can drive your organization to a higher and higher performance.

Be sure to investigate the best metric that will provide you the best value to manage your unique business needs. Just because somebody else is using a metric does not mean it will be the right metric for you.

Sample Financial KPIs

- Net Profit Margin
- Gross Profit Margin
- Operating Profit Margin
- EBITDA
- Return on Investment (ROI)
- Return on Capital Employed (ROCE)
- Return on Assets (ROA)
- Return on Equity (ROE)
- Debt-to-Equity (D/E) Ratio
- Working Capital Ratio

Sample Customer Related KPIs

- Customer Retention Rate
- Customer Satisfaction Index
- Customer Profitability Score
- Customer Lifetime Value
- Customer Turnover Rate
- Customer Engagement
- Customer Complaints

Sample Marketing KPIs

- Market Growth Rate
- Market Share
- Brand Equity
- Cost per Lead
- Conversion Rate
- Search Engine Rankings (by keyword) and Click-through Rate

- Page Views and Bounce Rate
- Customer Online Engagement Level
- Social Networking Footprint

Sample Operational KPIs

- Six Sigma Level
- Capacity Utilization Rate (CUR)
- Order Fulfilment Cycle Time
- On Time Delivery Rate
- Inventory Shrinkage Rate (ISR)
- Project Schedule Variance (PSV)
- Project Cost Variance (PCV)
- Earned Value (EV) Metric
- Rework Level
- Overall Equipment Effectiveness (OEE)
- Process or Machine Downtime Level

Sample Societal KPIs

- Carbon Footprint
- Water Footprint
- Energy Consumption
- Saving Levels Due to Conservation and Improvement Efforts
- Waste Reduction Rate
- Waste Recycling Rate
- Community Volunteer Hours
- Financial Contributions to Charity

Systematic Review Process

The processes, systems and recommendations I make in this book are all a waste if you don't implement a systematic review process. It is the Law of Entropy (order and disorder); if you don't put energy in it, your systems will decay and you'll be back into chaos. Schedule a time right now; put it on your calendar that you're going to review your metrics at least monthly. Be agile, add and delete as needed. I've been working the last several years with a division of ExxonMobil and I have been helping them establish metrics. Surprisingly, the department I have been helping had no metrics at all to start with, so we started looking at their key performance indicators and created a systematic process to review them.

We found that some of the metrics we developed weren't adding value, so we deleted it. We continued to look for new metrics that would better tell us what's going on in the organization and how we're improving (or not). Don't think it's going to be a one and done, develop metrics but be willing to take them out and move new ones in as required.

Visual Metrics

Be sure you find ways and locations to post your results. Be sure everyone can see what's going on in your organization. Break rooms and well-travelled halls are good examples, but post your charts, post your metrics and let employees know what's going on. I mentioned it before, I'll mention it again, make sure you go over these metrics in your monthly meetings with employees or maybe even in one-on-one meetings where you tell them how your department's going and how their own performance metrics are looking. Make sure that you keep it systematic and show metrics regularly. If you don't make it systematic, you're wasting your time.

Taking Action

Here are some action items to take away from this chapter:

- Work with your leadership team to develop your company's KPIs
- Create a process to make it systematic, show them monthly at a minimum
- Post your results for everyone to see
- Talk about metrics in employee meetings
- Benchmark with other organizations
- Develop a systematic review process and adjust as needed

Take all the results into a management review meeting and have your higher-level leadership team look at these and decide how you want to change things and how you can improve the organization.

Chapter 10
Effective Business Systems

This chapter is all about developing effective business systems. I am really looking forward to sharing this chapter with you because it's so important that we understand that our business is a series of systems and how we can use these systems to take the chaos out of our business and make it run much more effectively. Your understanding that your business is a system with a series of subsystems is what I consider to be a key in building a successful, sustainable business.

Let's get into the definition of a business system. Here's one of the best definitions I could find:

"A business system is a procedure, a process, a method, or a course of action that's designed to achieve a specific business result and that will ultimately benefit the customer."

It's very important that we build a system that runs itself. Here are just a few examples of business systems:

- Customer Systems
  - o Customer service
  - o Customer retention
  - o Employees

- o Hiring
- o Training
- Information Systems
  - o Computers/Network
- Accounting Systems
  - o Payroll
  - o Collections
  - o Purchasing
- Supplier System
  - o Supplier Selection
- Inventory Management Systems
- Marketing Systems
  - o Lead generation
  - o Sales conversion
  - o Pricing
- Operations
  - o Enterprise Resource Planning (ERP)
  - o Management Information System (MIS)
- Quality Systems
  - o Quality Control
- Distribution Systems

I really like this quote from Michael Gerber, "*Your company is a system. It's either a dysfunctional system or a functional system, but it is a system. Everything touches everything.*"

It's important to recognize that having an effective system will reduce chaos in your organization. I highly recommend that if you've not read *E-Myth*, you should do so immediately; every business owner should read *E-Myth*.

The Franchise Model

The franchise model is something that Michael Gerber talks a lot about in *E-Myth*. I think it's very important to understand because franchises offer some specific things, and even though that you may not be a franchise, you need to build these same kinds of things into your organization. The point Michael makes is that big franchise companies like McDonald's and others have tested business systems that are documented. Then they do a very good job of training everyone in the use of those systems.

It's interesting how McDonald's, for example, has organizations all over the world that follow the same processes to the letter. In fact, when I was in Tokyo, I had hamburgers at McDonald's that tasted exactly like the McDonald's here in the states. They teach a series of systems and they do it the same way everywhere. McDonalds can take a bunch of high school kids and produce the same results because they have built systems and train everyone in the system. It's a great model for you to understand the importance of a franchise type system. One of the things you can't miss about the franchise model is that they have the highest success rate of all start-up businesses. And I believe you can point to the fact that they have designed systems that have been proven that are the cause for such a high success rate.

There are secondary benefits of developing your organization to look more like a franchise, especially when it comes to building systems and documenting systems. While you are trying to document your processes and your systems, here's some things that you're going to find during the process. You're going to find areas that you can improve immediately.

You'll look at things and say, "Why do we do it that way?" And you'll improve them on the spot. Once you have a set of documented procedures, guidelines, processes, and systems, your employees will know exactly what's expected of them and they will have guidelines. In the end you've got some great, very effective training material. When you bring in a new employee you've got great training material to show them how we do it here. If processes break down, you can point them right back to the documented processes. It's so important that you document your process; it is an important part of building systems that are repeatable.

Quality System Advantages

Here are a few advantages of developing a quality system in your organization:

- You're going to have better consistency of the products and services
- A quality system reduces costly mistakes
- A quality system improves efficiency and productivity
- Once you put a quality system in place, you definitely will see improved customer satisfaction
- You will have in place a way of constantly improving your products and services
- These lead to improved financial performance
- Improved employee communications

What is Quality?

When we start talking about quality, you have to talk about some of the principles taught by Philip Crosby who is really the guru of the quality movement. He wrote a lot of books about quality including one called *Quality is Free*.

Here are some of the principles he taught about quality. This is what he called the four absolutes of quality.

- The first absolute is to understand that the definition of quality is conformance to requirements. It's not how good or perfect it is. Conformance to requirements is his definition of quality.
- The second absolute is that a system of quality is about prevention. It's not a quality appraisal system.
- The third absolute that he talked about so frequently is that the performance standard needed to be zero defects. There is no "that's close enough," for him.
- The fourth absolute that he taught was that the measurement of quality is the price of nonconformance. This means you need to know what it truly costs your organization to not put out a high-quality product or service and to be able to measure what that cost is to your organization.

Crosby's Fourteen Steps to Quality Improvement

Here's some more of the teachings of Philip Crosby and this one was called *The 14 Steps to Quality Improvement*.

1. It all started with management commitment. Without management commitment, you really can't move a quality initiative forward.
2. He believed in creating quality improvement teams, which back in that time period the term quality circles was very popular.

3. You have to measure your processes, which we talk about a lot in this book.

4. As already mentioned, you must understand the cost of quality.

5. You need to have real quality awareness in your organization.

6. You need to focus on correcting the problems, especially at the source.

7. You must have a way of monitoring your progress.

8. It's very important that you train your supervisors in quality systems.

9. He recommended that you have what's called a Zero Defects Day.

10. That you have well established improvement goals.

11. It is very important that you remove fear from the organization. Employees should have no fear at all of bringing quality issues, challenges and problems in the organization to you. You do not want your employees hiding quality issues, so you must remove fear from your organization.

12. As leaders you need to recognize the efforts of your employees to improve quality.

13. He put in what is called quality councils. This would be a group of employees that work together to improve quality in your organization.

14. Lastly, he recommended that you just repeat the cycle over and over.

These 14 steps are still used by many companies today.

ERP System

Another system I recommend you look into implementing in your organization is an ERP system. This stands for Enterprise Resource Planning. An ERP system is all about integrating your data across your organization. In this case, you might look for some industry-specific software that helps do this in your company. If you do purchase and install an ERP system, I want you to understand, it does take a lot of resources to put something like this in place. It is a very big project, so don't go into it blind. I wouldn't recommend putting in an ERP System if you're planning to sell your business in the next couple of years unless you know it will help increase the value of your business. It's kind of a long-term play but there's no doubt in my mind that an ERP System will help you run your business much more efficiently. If at some point in the future you do decide to sell your business, it will definitely impress a potential buyer. This is one of the things that I teach in my first book and subsequent training program *Business For Sale Blueprint*™.

As you can see in the graphic, an ERP system connects all your other systems: your inventory, production, accounting, human resources, delivery, business intelligence, sales, engineering, production planning, and purchasing. Again, it's a very big project, it is very challenging, but if you can link all these things together, you'll have a much more effective system.

Customer Satisfaction System

Here's a system I really like to recommend to all of my clients. You must have a deep understanding of your customer satisfaction. Here is the Customer Satisfaction System that I recommend to my clients.

It all starts with having a customer survey to get the pulse of your customer. A way of understanding exactly how your customer feels about the quality of your service and your products. After we have completed the customer survey and have the results, I like to put together some customer focus groups. Grab some of your key customers and then talk to them about the survey and say, "In this survey, we were rated fairly low on _____, why do you think that is? How could we improve?"

Get your customers involved in helping you figure out what you can do to improve your organization. Take your customer survey information into your annual strategic planning process and develop action plans around improving future results and increasing satisfaction levels. And then you start it all over again and you keep the cycle going. Every time you go through this cycle, you improve your company and improve customer satisfaction. It's an important process and I highly recommend you put something like this in place. In the quality industry this is called the "Voice of the Customer." Let the voice of the customer tell you how they perceive your company, the organization, your employees, processes, and the quality of your products and services.

Complaint Management System

Another system you should put into place in your organization is a complaint management system. I recommend that you create a tracking system for every customer complaint. It works best if you put one person in charge of reviewing and categorizing those complaints. Once they summarized, they can be discussed weekly in your management meetings. What you're looking for is trends. Do the complaints show you where you're going in your organization? Do you see a trend happening? It could be a trend up or down, but what you want to look for is trends. Next, add your complaint measurements into your metric system.

Don't view complaints negatively; contact your customers and thank them for bringing the complaint to your attention so that you can improve your business. You have to look at complaints as a positive. Be thankful customers said something so that you can learn about your organization and that you can work on improving it. Make a big deal of it and thank employees for pointing out issues.

Again, it goes back to one of Crosby's principles of taking away fear. If an employee knows that a customer is complaining about something, encourage them to bring that forward. Don't let them hide what's really happening in your organization. As I mentioned earlier, be sure to pull that information into your strategic planning and then develop strategies and action plans that will reduce or eliminate the complaints.

Another term for the Quality Teams that Philip Crosby talked about is what I call Process Improvement Teams. With Process Improvement Teams, you pull together a cross-section of your employees to work on a specific problem. Here are couple recommendations for you if you put together a Process Improvement Team.

- First, you want to be sure you answer any questions the team has about what they're supposed to be doing, what's the problem they're trying to solve, get those questions answered immediately.
- Create a team chart. This is a document that talks about what the team is supposed to do, what resources are allowed, how much time they're supposed to spend on it, and what they're trying to solve.

- Define the team roles. Who's going to do what on this team.

- Set the ground rules for the team.

- Be sure your team follows a systematic process. Again, the problem-solving process I recommend is the DMAIC process.

ISO 9000 System

Another system related to quality that you may want to put in place, depending on your organization, is an ISO 9000 system. This a great place to start with building a quality system. ISO 9000 has improved a lot over the years. When I first got involved in ISO, it was mostly a documentation process and you could document very poor processes. It has improved over the years to be a part of your whole management system, getting managers involved in a whole quality system. Look into ISO 9000 and the other ISO standards that relate to your industry.

Baldrige Award Criteria

Another system you should consider is the Malcolm Baldrige National Quality Award Criteria. Baldrige is a world-class system that encompasses the best practices of all successful businesses and the Baldrige award is administered by NIST (National Institute of Science and Technology). I love the Baldrige criteria. It breaks performance down into these seven categories.

1. Leadership - It all starts with leadership, without good leadership your organization of course will fail.

2. Strategic Planning - It's very important that you have a strong Strategic Planning Process.

3. Customer Focus - You must focus on the customer.

4. Measurement, Analysis, and Knowledge Management – You can't manage what you don't measure.

5. Workforce Focus - It's very important that you have a workforce focus. That you have a deep understanding of your employees, and their needs, and their satisfaction level.

6. Operations Focus – This would be all you operational systems that work together.

7. Results - If you do everything right in the top six categories, positive results will follow. The reverse is also true, if you're not doing a lot of things right in those top six categories, negative results will follow.

Read through the Baldrige Criteria. It will force you to ask a lot of very good, tough questions about your organization. As you read through it you'll say, "Oh, I've got a long way to go." The point is not to make you feel bad but rather learn where you need to improve.

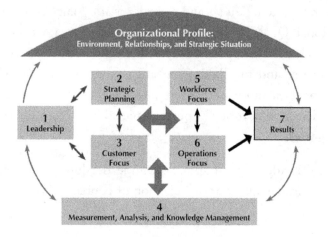

Here's a simple diagram in the Baldrige material that shows how these seven categories are all tied together. Something that is very important in the Baldrige criteria is how you go about maturing the process. You understand that in the beginning you're just reacting to problems. Next you move in to early systematic approaches where you start to get things lined up and you're starting to work towards strategic and operational goals. Next you start aligning your approaches and now you're being more strategic on how you handle your operational goals. Finally, you integrated all your approaches and now you're really reaching your strategic objectives. It's a very good model, it's very important to see your organization go through this transition, from reacting to problems to integrated approaches.

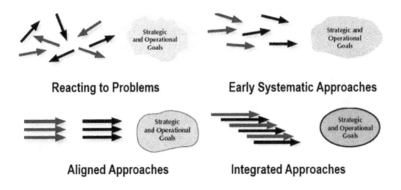

Reacting to Problems   **Early Systematic Approaches**

Aligned Approaches   **Integrated Approaches**

Documenting Processes

I talked earlier about the franchise model, and how franchises have documented all their processes. Let me talk a little bit more about documenting processes here. The first thing you need to do is create a list of your key processes. What are the most important processes in your organization? What I like to do is create a process map for each of those key processes. Then at a lower level, I'll write operating procedures that tie in to each of the key processes. Next you must create a place to store your documents so they can be readily available to your team. Another key though to documenting your processes is having a system to keep them updated and that your procedures stay current. If you don't have a process of keeping them current, you actually could be wasting your time in even documenting in the first place.

Process Mapping

Let's talk about what a process is. The definition, really, of a process is *"A series of actions or activities that are performed to achieve a desired output or result"*. Every process has an input and an output. There's an input to the process and an output to the process. Process mapping is a great tool for documenting key processes.

Here's me at ExxonMobil where they had great giant whiteboards where I am developing a process map for one of their divisions.

What is a Process?

- A process is a series of actions or activities that are performed to achieve a desired output or result.
- Every process has an input and an output.

- All process outputs should be measurable.
- Process mapping is a method used to gain awareness of an organization's procedures and analyze them to identify sources of:
  - o Errors
  - o Defects
  - o Inefficiencies
- A process map makes the process more visible and simpler to comprehend to all those involved in the process.
- Process maps can be constructed at both micro and macro levels, depending on the level or the degree of detailing.

I recommend you identify the key processes in your business and begin the creation of Process Maps for each of them.

There are a series of standard symbols used in Process Mapping that you need to become familiar with. These symbols are available on Microsoft products like Word, Excel, and Visio. This becomes a standard language that helps everyone visualize the performance. I prefer Visio but you can create effective Process Maps with Word and Excel. The following are a few common symbols:

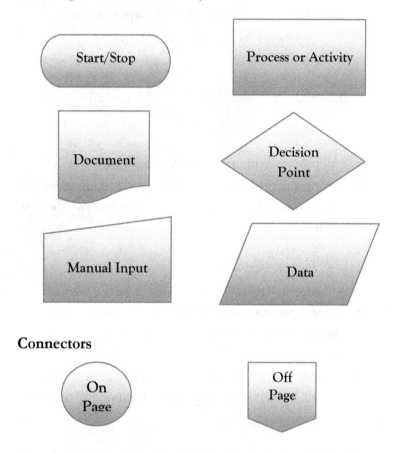

Connectors

Google "Process Maps" and you will obtain hundreds of great examples.

I highly recommend you use what's called a Deployment Style Process Map, or sometimes also called a Cross Functional Process Map. And this is where you put your process map in what we call swim lanes. Here's an example of a process map that might have multiple swim lanes and they can be at different levels. For example, you might have the first swim lane for the customer, but the next interaction might be with an accounts payable clerk. Then another swim lane could be the office manager, then it might be a supplier, and there could be a warehouse. You see how we can go from a broad audience to maybe even a more individual audience or then to a department.

Customer
Accounts Payable Clerk
Production Manager
Vendor/Supplier
Warehouse

Here's an example of a deployment style process map that I did for one of my clients:

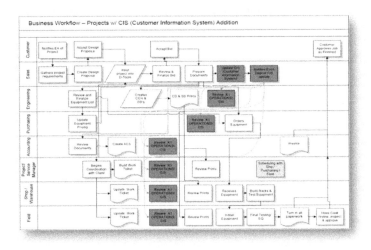

On a side note, in two hours of meetings with a team of six employees at my client's office, we created a revised process the client calculated would save them over $17,000 per year in labor costs. This is a great example of how while you are building process maps, you can often identify areas of improvement. While mapping, someone is bound to ask, "Why do we do it this way?" which is your opportunity to improve the process and save money immediately.

Now it is your turn; the following are some recommendations:

- Pull together a Process Mapping Team
- On a flip chart or white board, visualize and draw the process
- Be careful to keep it simple and stay away from unnecessary detail
- Analyze the details before including it on the computer
- Show the finished Process Map to someone unfamiliar with the process and see how well they understand it

Value Stream Mapping

Now, I'd also like to mention another process mapping style which is called Value Stream Mapping. This is process mapping on steroids. It has a lot of additional symbols that you add to your process map that will give you a better indication of what's going on.

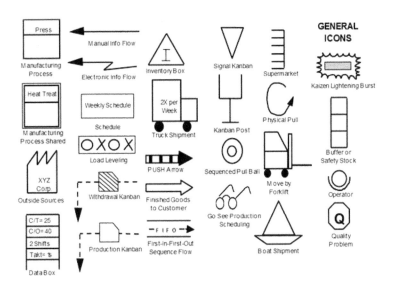

This is used a lot in Lean Manufacturing Methodology. It shows how the communication flows as well as how the products flow through an organization. Here's an example of a value stream map that I did for a client.

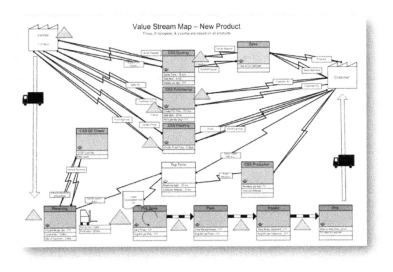

Just Google Value Stream Mapping and there are a lot of really good sources of information out there that will help you learn how to do this.

Document Control System

When I talked earlier about creating documents, I mentioned that you must develop a way to control your documents and keep them current. That's called a Document Control System and here are some recommendations around that:

- Have a central location to store all this corporate knowledge. Now, in the digital age, there's probably a place in a SharePoint site or on your server somewhere where you're storing all of your information. If a lot of your documents are manual, you have a place for that as well.

- Make sure it's easy for your employees to retrieve the documents so that they can get their hands on the documents quickly.

- Make sure you've got security in place for your critical documents. Of course, every organization is different, but you might have some documents that are very sensitive. Certainly, your HR documents are very critical, but you might have other documents that require additional security, especially when it comes to maybe things like medical records and that type of thing.

- Make sure that you can pull documents quickly for employees that are new and in training.

- You'll find that having a good document control system will help you in meeting compliance requirements, especially any kind of audit that might happen in your organization.

- A good document control system is very important in disaster recovery, so you do want to keep this in mind and make sure you have an off-location place where you can get your hands on your documents. Possibly, make sure your documents are all stored in the Cloud, so in the event of a disaster, you can get your hands on them quickly.

- A document control system ensures that you're systematic about your processes and procedures.

This type of system will make sure that you maintain the most current processes and documents. And a good document control system will reduce the waste of looking for or recreating documents and procedures.

Lean/Six Sigma

While on the subject of systems that could be important to your organization, I have to mention Lean/Six Sigma. Lean is a system that's developed primarily by Toyota that was designed to remove waste from processes. Six Sigma was a system first developed by Motorola to reduce or eliminate defects. Both of these together offer very effective tools to help improve performance in your organization. I have a Lean/Six Sigma Black Belt Certification which helps me bring these two systems together to work on removing waste and eliminating defects together at the same time for my clients.

I hope you recognized from this chapter how important it is to view your business as a system and a series of subsystems and to really work on improving the systems in your organization.

Taking Action

Here are some action items to take away from this chapter:

- If you haven't already, read *E-Myth* by Michael Gerber.
- Make a list of all the systems that make up your business. Be sure you've got a handle on all the systems and subsystems.
- Take a look at ISO 9000 or the Baldrige model. They can help you identify systems and processes in your organization that maybe you didn't look at before or think of as a system.
- Implement a complaint management system. This will feed into a lot of other systems and help you improve the overall organization.
- Begin now to document all your processes and procedures.
- Create a document control system that will keep all those records current and easily accessible for your employees.
- Take a look at Lean Six Sigma principles and see how they might reduce waste or improve quality in your company.

There's a lot of really good information available on developing systems in your organization to improve your company. This chapter is simply giving you a high-level overview. I'm not recommending that you try to do all this right away; I'm just giving you an overview of some of the things you might be able to put into place in your organization. You can't do it all, be sure and take baby steps. If you see some systems that you really need to put in place but don't have the resources on staff to do it, look outside, look for some resources that can come in and help you put in systems that can make a difference immediately in your company.

Chapter 11
Continuous Transformation

I'm sure you recognize how fast things are changing in our world. Technology is changing everything and the pace of change is staggering. We have to develop a continuous improvement process and mindset in our organization, a culture of continuous transformation. We'll talk here about making that a part of your culture. I believe a business leader that fails to create a culture that embraces change and seeks innovation is destined to mediocrity at best and really complete failure at the worst.

Speed of Change

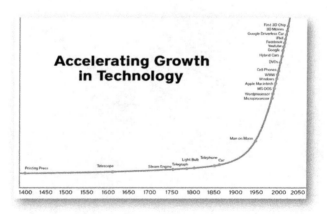

None of us can deny that change has happened faster and faster. I love this chart and the way it visually displays the growth of technology. Obviously, the increase in technology started about the time we put the man on the moon. Now, technology changes daily. This chart makes it very clear that change is not going to slow down and we're going to have to be prepared to deal with rapid changes.

- Are you looking into the future when it comes to what changes are happening and the speed of change?
- How current are you with your industry's new technologies?
- How well have you and your team adapted to the recent technology changes?
- Are you trying to get by with old, outdated machinery and software?
- Are you looking into the future as a part of your regular strategic planning process?

Leading the Charge

In strategic planning, it's very important to look into the future. As a leader, what kind of example are you? I've known many business owners and leaders that want their employees to adapt to changing technologies, but refuse to do so themselves. I believe that effective handling of the changes in your business starts with you at the leadership level. Your attitude makes all the difference. Do you fear change yourself or are you embracing it? You should make agility and innovation a core value of your company. A great place where you can show leadership here is to reward and recognize your team for exhibiting agility and the appropriate response to changes.

Changes in your organization, in your industry, and in your business environment.

Change Management

There are whole industries that have sprung up around change management and change management professionals. I'll just cover some of the basics here. You can definitely take a deep dive into this and learn a lot more about dealing with change management in your company. Change management is all about effectively addressing the human side. As I just mentioned, it all starts at the top.

It's very important that you get everyone involved. You have to paint the value proposition. You must explain to your employees why you're changing so that they can understand and get behind the changes that are needed in your organization. You also must communicate, communicate, and communicate. If you think you're communicating already too much, you probably aren't. As you work through change management processes, be prepared for resistance. We know people resist change but there are ways to effectively deal with employees and their resistance. You must be aware that change will require patience on your part and your leadership team's part. This may be an area that you need some outside expertise, some coaching or some training to help you if you're dealing with some very large changes in your organization.

A great little book that I recommend that can help you and your employees deal with change is called *Who Moved My Cheese?* A very low-cost strategy that I recommend is that you buy your employees a copy of the book and then you have weekly meetings or lunch and learns where you talk about the book, talk about how it applies to your company, and talk about the different strategies in this book. It gives your employees freedom to discuss change and how they're dealing with it. It's a great little tool.

Here are some principles that are taught in the book:

- Change happens
- You have to anticipate change
- You monitor change
- Adapt to change quickly
- Then change
- Now you enjoy change
- Be ready to change quickly and enjoy it all over again.

It's a fun read about four mice dealing with change and the fact that their cheese has been moved. It's a great tool and I highly recommend you use it.

Continuous Improvement Culture

It's essential that you create an environment where improvement, transformation, and innovation are the norm. Employees should begin to expect that and understand that that's part of their job, and that's just the way it is in your organization. The more they understand "that's just the way it is," the less they'll resist it. I recommend that you make it a part of your company's core values and then set goals that link to this value. It's very important that you train employees in problem solving skills. Problem solving skills really help them adapt to change better and figure out ways to work through the change process. The more they're a part of the change process, the more they'll buy into it. That's so much better than just throwing the change at them and saying, "Here it is, deal with it!" Get them involved in the problem solving and creating new change processes and really make it a team effort.

I've mentioned these before but there are tools that can help you as you work on a continuous improvement system. First, there's Lean/Six Sigma. That's all about improving processes, reducing waste. Lean/Six Sigma is all about change. It's all about improving processes, removing waste, and about removing defects. It helps you walk through a change process. I also mentioned earlier the Baldrige Criteria which can also help in creating a culture of change. Also, ISO 9000 has some great change elements in it. What I like is a hybrid approach. I will grab parts of Lean/ Six Sigma, Baldrige and ISO, and put them together for what fits the company. Create a hybrid approach and use the tools that best fit your organization.

DMAIC Problem Solving Process

I mentioned it before, but I feel strongly you should teach your team some problem-solving skills and I highly recommend the DMAIC Problem Solving Process. Let me go in a little bit more detail about it here.

- The **D** stands for **Define** the problem. It all starts with understanding what the problem is and getting your arms around that.

- **M** is for **Measure** - We have to measure the current state. If we don't know the current state, we won't know whether we've improved it or not. Get a measurement of the current state. Then take a deep dive and analyze the root causes. What's causing the current state?

- **I** stands for Improve - Here, you implement a solution that you believe will solve or improve the problem.

- **C** stands for **Control** and you control it by measuring results.

This is at a very high level, but I wanted you to have an understanding what DMAIC stands for. There are some really good books and training available on DMAIC and other systematic problem-solving approaches.

Management Has Changed

We really can't manage the way we did in the past. I'm sure you have also recognized that employee values have changed. Obviously, we've already mentioned technology has greatly changed but people have also changed. Phrases like, "Because I'm the boss," never really was an effective management tool and is even less effective now. We've already talked about how important communication is, but the old style of management kept things close to the vest and didn't have communication with your employees. That does not work anymore, you must communicate.

One thing that really has to change is we can no longer afford to put people in leadership that aren't properly trained. To go a step further with that, we can't put people in leadership that really don't have the right skillset or the right attitudes about leadership. I have been in so many organizations that have put people into supervisor or leadership roles, just because there were good at a skill. Many sales managers started off as a really good salesperson but when they were put into a sales management role, they flopped.

That's just one example. I've seen it in every industry and in every type of employee. You take somebody that's pretty good at something and say, "Hey, we'll make you a manager." They didn't train them to be a manager and they really weren't suited to be a manager. They were destined to fail. Don't do that. Don't put people in leadership positions that aren't ready for it and aren't trained for it. That's one of the biggest problems I consistently see in management. If I can convince you to change anything, I really hope you change that. Be much more systematic about putting people in leadership positions. And if you made some mistakes in the past and you've got people in leadership right now, give them proper training and then if they don't have the right attitude or the skillsets to be a leader, gracefully find a way to move them into another position and put somebody else in the leadership role. It's painful and you might hurt some feelings, but it needs to be done.

I think we have to recognize that different generations have some different mindsets. I recognize that I'm painting with a broad brush and I know there are exceptions, but I think most people agree these are generally true. For example, I'm a Baby Boomer. Baby Boomers are competitive and they think workers should pay their dues. Gen Xers, this is a group from 1965 to 1977. They're more likely to be very skeptical and independent minded. We now have what's called Gen Ys, also known as millennials. They're born 1978 and later and they like teamwork, feedback and technology. One of the things I've noticed about the younger generation is they're not as motivated by money as some of the past generations. They like having time off. They're more motivated by freedom and flexibility and a fun place to work. Very different from the Baby Boomer generation.

Let me make a few recommendations around how management has changed. Teach your leaders how to recognize the difference, not only generational, but differences in personality. How do you manage different personalities effectively? I think it's very important to facilitate mentoring between ages. Team an older person up with a younger person. You may be surprised at how well they work together. If at all possible, offer different working options. If you can, let them work from home from time to time and let them have a flex schedule if at all possible.

You need to learn how to accommodate different learning styles. Everybody learns differently. You need to make sure that you accommodate all the learning styles in your training and the way you work with your employees. And you must keep your employees engaged and with a voice. What I mean by "with a voice" is that you have a system in place to hear their concerns, their needs, and they know that you're listening and that you hear them. Being heard is simply a human need that we all have. Find ways to accommodate employee's personal needs. The better you are at accommodating their personal needs, the more they know you care and that you value them as an employee.

My last recommendation here is to create some sort of recognition program, be sure you let employees know how valuable they are to you. Be sure that you recognize your employees for their willingness to change, agility and innovative charge. Also let employees know how much you appreciate their willingness to improve processes and improve the way you meet customer expectations.

Taking Action

Here are some action items to take away from this chapter:

- Recognize the fast changes going on in your industry and address those in your planning.
- Lead by example, be the one that starts the culture shift in your organization.
- Study change management. I gave you a real high-level overview here, but I recommend you study more about change management and read up on it, this will really help you get started.
- Look for a continuous improvement structure that works best for your organization.
- Train every employee in problem solving skills like DMAIC.
- Teach your managers how to manage the generational differences and to how do it effectively.

Let me remind you here that I've just covered a lot of information and some of this takes years to perfect. Remember, you can't do it all. Pick a few items that you can do now and then come back to these chapters over and over again. Each time you read this, you'll get more and more ideas that you can implement. I want to share effective strategies with you here and let you pick where to start and what works best for you and your company. As I have mentioned before, I don't expect to you put all this into place right away. You do have to pick and choose here, but I would be doing you a disservice if I just picked a couple for you and didn't share all the different strategies and ideas that might be effective for your company. Be very discriminative here and work with your team to find out what works best for you.

Chapter 12
Funding the Turnaround

This chapter is about finding the resources needed to fund your turnaround. Like the other chapters, it's at a very high level and designed to give you some things to think about as you look for ways to fund your turnaround.

I think a great analogy for turning around a failing business is a wilderness survival situation. You must be willing to eat bugs and you have to focus on the basics: food, water and shelter. For your business, this means taking some unpleasant actions and focusing back on business basics. That's really what we've talked about throughout this whole book. Getting back to the basics, doing the things you must do to survive.

You really have two sources for finding funds in your turnaround. The first source is internal. We'll talk about cost-cutting, improving your revenue and we'll talk about reserves. Then, you have external funding. I will cover getting accounts receivable loans, loan restructuring, and a little bit about investors and partnerships. Lastly, we will discuss whether selling your business might be an option to consider.

INTERNAL FUNDING

Cost-Cutting

I have covered cost-cutting in some of the previous chapters but I'm going to repeat it again here as we focus on how we're going to find lost cash to turn around your business. Here are some of the things where it is like eating bugs, things that are very unpleasant but need to be considered. I recommend that you lay off all non-essential personnel. You may need to get your core team down to those who are essential to running your business and meeting current customer expectations. You may not be in a position to have excess staff for the possible surges in your business. Get down to a core staff that can handle your current business load. I have seen so many businesses struggling (and I have been there myself) that hold on to the "what if get busy and don't have enough staff" thinking. Focusing on saving the company and you can deal with business surges in the future.

When some industries take a downturn you not only see them lay off a percentage of their workforce but they will implement pay cuts for those who were remaining. It's very common to let pay and salaries get above the market and then have a hard time cutting people back. Now might be the perfect time to get your salaries in line with the industry and the current marketplace.

This may seem like a very small item, but I've seen a lot of money wasted on office supplies. Here's a place where you can cut those costs and also send a message that we're going to look at every cost in the organization.

If you're like many companies, cellphone costs are huge. If at all possible, cut out the use of cellphones. I recognize that may not be possible in some industries or business models. It may also be time to consider cutting out all company cars. If you have a lot of money going to company vehicles, this may be a cost-cutting area for you to review.

I recommend that you remove credit cards from everyone. You may keep a credit card for yourself and some key employees that you can trust that you know will only use the card in emergencies. But you must get control of how your cash is being spent in your company, now.

Another place to cut costs is to renegotiate your building lease. This can be a very effective tool. You may be surprised to find that a landlord could be willing to negotiate and give you a break on your lease, especially if part of the reason for your downturn is a poor economy. You may be in a better negotiating position with your landlord than you realize. It is also possible that your lease rates have increased higher than the market will bear. Be sure you look at this option and even take time to look at where you could move that would lower your overall overhead. Maybe you don't really need the space you once did or planned to need.

This won't apply to everyone, but if you buy a lot of marketing materials: pens, notepads, coffee mugs, promotional items, etc., it might be a time to cut back on those and keep that cash for more essential items.

Cut back on travel. Don't travel at all if you can avoid it. If you or your team has to travel, go on the cheap. I have seen many cases where travel could be eliminated or reduced with video conferencing.

Take a look at your equipment leases. Do you have leases on equipment like machinery, copiers, etc.? Do you have equipment leases that you just really don't need, especially if your company and your sales are down? Do you really have to have those leases? This might be a place where you can cut costs substantially. I helped an ExxonMobil division with a MPS (Managed Print Services) project that cut copier, printer and printer cartridge cost by over $500,000 per year. This is an often-overlooked expense area.

Look for ways to reduce your shipping costs. Cut out overnight deliveries as much as possible, look for cheaper carriers. Possibly add a few extra days to your promised delivery date for your customers so you can go with the lower cost of ground freight.

If you're in a very tight cash flow, now is not the time to be philanthropic. I would recommend you eliminate contributions. Even if you've given to certain charities year after year, you may have to consider cutting back now. Again, we're talking survival mode, and you have to make decisions that are based on your current situation. Eliminate these kinds of costs wherever you can.

Look to see if you could sublease some of your extra space (some leases may not allow it). Maybe you've leaned down, you don't need as much space as you did a year or so ago. Especially if sales are down, and you've done some of the things I've talked about, about cutting inventory and removing a lot of wasted inventory. Sublease some of that extra space out, it might be a way of generating some extra cash.

These are just a few ideas that you might look into in order to cut costs. As I mentioned with the other chapters, do zero-based thinking. You have to really think about what do you really need to survive and to run your business. Try to eliminate all those costs that don't lead to the survival and the success of your business. We're talking turnaround here, we're talking about survival. We want to save the business and we want it to come out on the other side of this stronger than it ever was. These are good disciplines to put in place.

Increasing Revenue

I highly recommend you consider increasing your prices. I know this will come as a shock to you. You may be thinking, "Hey, I'm in survival mode, how could I ever raise my prices? I would lose all my customers." Well, you need to study pricing strategy. Many business owners have found they can raise their prices and not lose business at all. If you're giving your customers great value, great service, then you should consider your pricing strategy. A small increase in prices can give you an immediate increase in profitability.

Look into how you can reactivate old customers. I once had a client that had been in business 20 years and never once reached out to their old customers to try to get new business from them. Dig out your customer list and look for customers you haven't talked to or heard from for a long time. Reach out to them and find out how they're doing and if there is anything else you can do to help them. If you're like most businesses there's a goldmine in your old customer list.

I mentioned this under inventory, but I'll mention it again. Sell all old and excess inventories and get rid of it. You may have to take 10 cents on the dollar, but it's better than it sitting in your warehouse. Another strategy is to offer old inventory to your clients at a much-reduced rate. They get a good deal and you get it out of your inventory.

Consider changing your payment policies. I talked about this before, where you might raise your prices a little bit, but then offer a discount back to your normal price for payment in advance. This can help your cash flow immensely. This is great strategy that I've used myself multiple times and it did wonders at bringing in extra cash quickly. You may want to enact some sort of changes in your payment policies, especially payments in advance as much as possible. Maybe you're giving credit to people that you shouldn't be, but maybe also you could ask for 50% down and 50% on delivery, especially if you're giving your customer some sort of special bonus or discount. You can say, "Hey, with this discount I need different payment terms." Hey, it doesn't hurt to ask and nobody will fault you for asking.

Giving bonuses for early payment is a strategy I've used multiple times and it's been very effective on improving cash flow. What I actually do is raise the prices slightly and then discount back to my original price for early payment or even pre-payment. Of course, every business is different, but try this if it fits in your industry and in your market. I actually learned this strategy from the US Government. I was doing some Government projects and they, actually, at the time encouraged that. They always looked at the discounted price for bid selection, as opposed to the marked-up price. Be sure to use it if at all possible.

I've mentioned this before, but if you have money out on accounts receivable, you must collect it aggressively. Be the squeaky wheel. Call those clients, get in touch with them, ask them when the check is going to be here. You need to be aggressive. You are not a bank. You're not in the business of loaning money to your clients. If they're having cash flow problems, don't let them pass that on to you. What it really does is cause a domino effect. They slow pay you, and then now you have to slow pay your vendors and then they... it just goes on, and on, and on. Be aggressive. Get that cash in as quickly as possible.

I'm not a tax expert, but here is a strategy around taxes that you should talk to your CPA about. The first thing you should do is reduce your tax payments to match your current year projections. So if you had a good last year and you're down this year in sales and profitability, make sure you're not making the same kind of quarterly tax payments as you did last year. Another thing to talk to your CPA about is if you're projecting a loss this year, talk to them about filing the return right away to get a loss carry back. Be sure to let your CPA know what your situation is, and they may have other strategies and ideas to help you.

Here I want to talk about reserves. I recognize the possibility that you've used up all your reserves, if you had any, and you're not in a position to really build up reserves right now. But it's pretty obvious that the best way to fund a turnaround is to have planned well enough in advance for the inevitable downturns that happen in every industry and every business and that you have reserves that can help you in those lean times. If you're just now making the turn, make an effort to start building up reserves for that next downturn in your industry. But the first step is what we've talked about earlier about cutting costs. Keep those cost-cutting efforts into effect.

EXTERNAL FUNDING

This section will give you some ideas, food for thought, and offer a little advice along the way.

My first piece of advice about external funding is:

USE EXTREME CAUTION!

While obtaining external funding can be a strategy that could save your business, it can also be one of those things that'll take your business down. Try everything possible to reduce expenses and increase revenue before considering getting external funding. I'm speaking from experience. I had to close down a business many years ago and lose everything, and a contributing factor was external loans. I'll emphasize this one more time; I believe it's important that you look within your own organization to find the funding resources for your turnaround. Using external sources should be considered only as a last resort to save your business. I can't drive that home enough.

Accounts Receivable Loans

Getting a loan against Accounts Receivable is the first and most common place business owners look to get some external funding. I recommend you only consider a receivables loan when your bank will not give you a line of credit based on your assets. Accounts receivable loans are also called factoring and it's actually selling your receivables. They take on most of the risk but you still hold some of the risk yourself. Here are some of the pros of getting an accounts receivable loan:

- It's fast cash and you get some working capital immediately.
- It's based on your customers' ability to pay and not yours, which is a good thing if you're really in a tight situation.
- You are not required to give up any collateral (the receivables are the collateral).
- You don't have to give up any business ownership in this scenario.

Some of the cons against selling your receivables to another company are:

- May cause some concerns for your customer, just because of the perception that this is a sign that you're in trouble.
- It is more costly (higher interest) than your standard business loan rate.
- Factoring companies may not want to accept any of your past-due receivables. This could leave you with a lot of receivables on your books that they won't accept.
- Funding companies are all different, but it's possible uncollected funds may come back on you, so you only really want to factor receivables from customers that have a solid payment history.

Also, make sure you are even allowed to get an Accounts Receivable. If you have a SBA or bank loan, they could be stipulations that you can't sell of receivables to a third party. Do your due diligence.

Loan Restructuring

This is a cost-cutting and cash flow improvement effort with your external lender. You must be communicating your situation to your lender. I talked about this in the chapter Communication with your Key Stakeholders. You must take responsibility for communication, especially if you've been in a mode where you haven't let them know what's going on. You need to show them your turnaround strategy, show them what you're doing, and show them the actions you've already taken to turn around your company. You must understand their position and their needs. It's not personal, it's business.

Here are a few possible restructuring options to talk with your lender about:

- Extending the maturity date; a loan that's coming due in the next six months might be moved out a year or two until your cash flow is better. That could help you keep from having to come up with the funds to close out a loan.

- Ask if you could go interest-only for a while and not have to pay principal. This could help your cash flow immensely.

- Request a period of time where you can defer principal and interest both. Of course, interest will continue to pile up, but maybe you could ask for the next three months or six months without making a payment at all.

The bank would rather do that often than see you default on the loan.

- Ask for a reduced interest rate. It's possible that you got the loan at a time when interest was much higher. Look at what the current market rate should be for interest and ask for a reduced rate.

- It may be a long shot, but you could actually ask for some forgiveness for principal and past-due interest.

It'll definitely depend on your situation, the kind of relationship you have with your lending institution.

Investors

Another source for funding might be bringing in investors. It is possible you could find some investors who'll give you some cash for either equity in your business or just a high return on investment. This strategy may be ideal in some situations, but the risk might outweigh the actual rewards.

Here are some pros and cons of finding what's called an Angel Investor. There's a lot of money out there on the market to be invested but it comes with pros and cons. Some of the pros:

- They may have deep pockets that can quickly bail you out of your current situation.

- They might have business experience that can help you and some connections that can really improve your business.

Some of the cons are:

- It can take you a long time to find the ideal investor.

- They may want a high rate of return, as much as 25%, or even more.

- They might even require that you give up some control of your business or even some owner equity.

If you choose to go after an investor, I first want to recommend that you read *Pitch Anything* by Oren Klaff. This is a very good book that talks about the psychology of pitching a deal. I can guarantee you that if I were going to an investor to ask for money, I would use the principles taught in the *Pitch Anything* book or his on-line program.

Bringing on a Partner

You may want to consider bringing on a partner but as we have seen before, there are pros and cons here, as well. Here are some pros:

- You may find a partner that has funds to buy a percentage interest of your business, and they can bring some cash into your company.

- You might find a partner that has business experience that could add to your organization.

- A partner could share the burden. I had a partner for 14 years, and I know the pros and cons, but I know the advantages of having a partner to share the burden and ease the pressure on you.

- A partner can provide accountability. They can help you from going too far out on a limb in one direction.

- Partners are great to bounce ideas off and help you evaluate some of the strategies. The old saying is true that "two heads are better than one."

Some cons are:

- Like some of the other strategies, it could take a long time to find the ideal partner.

- Obviously, if you take on a partner, you're going to have to give up some ownership.

- There's a real risk that your partner won't have the same vision for the organization as you do, and may want to move your company in a completely different direction.

- While there's a chance your partner might bring some of the skills you need, also the reverse is true, they may be lacking in the skills that your business needs.

- Obviously, you're going to have to start sharing the profitability. If you were already low on profitability, and now you've got to share profits with someone else, at whatever percentage, this could hurt your cash flow and hurt you personally.

- Your new partner may want to come in and want to work in the day-to-day operations of your business and expect a salary. This would increase your payroll and your owner-cash draw, also hurting cash flow.

- There's the legal responsibility associated with having partners, and you can be responsible for the actions of your partners.

This will just give you some things to think about. There are pros and cons in every situation. Don't take this decision lightly. The problem we face is, when we are in a tough situation, we're stressed, cash flow is poor, and our business is failing, we don't always make the right decisions. We begin thinking that taking on a partner, getting an angel investor, getting some cash in from one of those sources, an external source, will save everything. It's not always the answer and it can make things worse. Get some advice and make sure you're making the right decision.

Selling the Business

Let me talk for a minute about selling your business. You may be so burnt out by now and in such a financial stress, that you just want to sell your business and get out. I have been there myself, and I have had clients that were there. You can get to the point where you just don't have the energy and the mindset needed to struggle any further and turn around your business. While this is an option you could consider, if you're in a downturn, this is the worst possible time to try to sell a business. Now, of course, it's better than filing bankruptcy and losing everything, but you may be lucky to come out with any money at all.

You see, selling a business is not an easy bet, and I guarantee you that. It could take you many, many months. If your business is not profitable that's going to dramatically reduce the value of your business. Your business valuation is based on profitability and cash flow. If you're in tight cash flow you are not going to see much value for your business, in the eyes of a prospective buyer. The other thing that happens when you try to sell a business, is you spend a great deal of time with tire-kickers. They come in, they want to see your financials, they look at your business, you get your hopes up, you invest a lot of time, and then the next thing you know, they're onto something else and you've been standing there thinking you might have had a deal coming. What happens here, too, is you're so focused on the buyers, you stop running your business and you stop working on improving your business. Don't let that happen to you. Even if you start looking for a buyer, make sure you're doing all the strategies we talk about in this book.

The truth is 79% of the businesses that go on the market fail to sell. You see, I know a little bit about selling your business, because I have even written a book on it, *Business For Sale Blueprint*, and created on on-line training program on it by the same name. If you do decide to go the route of selling your business, take a look at this training, but it's not an easy button. It can be a long road, and so, do the other strategies that we talk about in this program.

Taking Action

Here are some action items to take away from this chapter:

- The first thing you do, is you cut costs wherever possible. Remember, it may feel like eating bugs, but this is survival.

- After you get through this period, start thinking about what you're going to do about building reserve savings after you get through this period. You need a way of protecting yourself from the next storm. There will always be another storm, don't forget that.

- If you are looking at external funding sources, be very cautious, weigh all the pros and cons. And again, this is just my recommendation, but I would take on investors or partners only as a last resort to save your business.

Everything I have shared here is my opinion and based on my personal experience. I feel it's my obligation to share with you those things that might help you avoid potential negative situations. I want you to be able to look back and realize that having gone through this challenge has made your business stronger and more profitable.

Conclusion

Congratulations. I applaud your efforts to read this book and focus on improving your business. You have completed the 12 chapters of Business Turnaround Blueprint. We have covered a lot of information together. It's like drinking out of a fire hose; drink what you can, but come back again and again to get more because you can't get it all at once.

One thought that I've tried to hit home in every single chapter is that none of this will be of any value if you don't take action. Action is the name of the game, that's where it is. You have to develop a process of implementing and taking action on all these items that you realize you must do to improve your business. Go back through your notes. Review the chapters again. I recommend you put a sticky note on your computer that says, 'action'. This is the one thing you have to do to turn around a struggling business; you have to take action, you have to take the appropriate actions at the appropriate time, but take action.

I wish you great success and I look forward to hearing from you about how this book has helped you turn around or simply improve your business.

Fred Herbert

P.S. Get additional resources at:

www.BusinessTurnaroundBlueprint.com/book-resources

How I Help My Clients

I am absolutely confident that you could take everything we covered in this book and on your own put it into action and get results that you thought previously weren't possible. I am certain the with the information we've covered here, with your own resources, time and effort you can turnaround your business in a way the most people would never be able to do.

And if that were you only option it would be worth pursuing.

But this is another option. An option where you and I could work together.

What if I played an active role in helping you get results, took a responsibility in your success and had an obligation to your outcome? How would that make things different?

Do you think in that situation I could empower you with any and all resources at my disposal to stack the deck in your favor?

If that option was available to you, would you love to hear about it and what it could do for you?

That's why it's is with great pleasure that I introduce to you, the **"Business Turnaround Blueprint A.P.E. Program"**

Here is briefly how I work with clients:

Step 1: Assessment

I work closely with you to do a completely unbiased **Strategic Business Assessment** of your business to get to the truth of your current situation. Contact me to learn more about the 15 areas covered **Strategic Business Assessment** and how you can use it in your **Strategic Planning Process** and for overall business improvement.

Step 2: Planning

We now take the assessment of your business and help you develop a Turnaround Plan to take you from the current state to the desired future state.

Step 3: Execution

Here we work together to build an **Execution System** that ensures the plan will be implemented and systematically reviewed and adjusted along the way.

Here it the link to get on my calendar to discuss your current business situation and determine if my program would be right for you.

www.fredherbert.com/schedule

I wish you every success and look forward to hearing how these strategies have impacted your business and your life.

CPSIA information can be obtained
at www.ICGtesting.com
Printed in the USA
LVHW080054270721
693782LV00012B/787